WINDOWS® 95
QUICK REFERENCE

Written by Janice A. Snyder

Windows 95 Quick Reference

Library of Congress Catalog No.: 97-65035

ISBN: 0-7897-1105-2

99 98   6 5 4 3 2

Interpretation of the printing code: the rightmost double-digit number is the year of the book's printing; the rightmost single-digit number, the number of the book's printing. For example, a printing code of 97-1 shows that the first printing of the book occurred in 1997.

Credits

PRESIDENT
Roland Elgey

PUBLISHER
Joseph B. Wikert

PUBLISHING DIRECTOR
David W. Solomon

EDITORIAL SERVICES DIRECTOR
Elizabeth Keaffaber

MANAGING EDITOR
Thomas F. Hayes

ACQUISITIONS MANAGER
Elizabeth South

ACQUISITIONS EDITOR
Angela Wethington

SENIOR PRODUCT DIRECTOR
Lisa D. Wagner

PRODUCT DEVELOPMENT SPECIALIST
Dana S. Coe

SERIES DESIGN COORDINATOR
Caroyln Kiefer

PRODUCTION EDITOR
Sarah Rudy

PRODUCT MARKETING MANAGER
Kris Ankney

ASSISTANT PRODUCT MARKETING MANAGERS
Karen Hagen
Christy M. Miller

TECHNICAL EDITOR
Keith Underdahl

TECHNICAL SUPPORT SPECIALIST
Nadeem Muhammed

ACQUISITIONS COORDINATOR
Tracy M. Williams

OPERATIONS COORDINATORS
Patty Brooks
Susan Gallagher

EDITORIAL ASSISTANT
Virginia Stoller

BOOK DESIGNER
Ruth Harvey

COVER DESIGNER
Nathan Clement

PRODUCTION TEAM
Brian Grossman
Daryl Kessler
Steph Mineart
Lisa Stumpf

INDEXERS
Sandra Henselmeier
Nadia Ibrahim

Composed in *Century Old Style* and *Franklin Gothic* by Que Corporation.

To my Dad, Al Nielsen, the book you need to make most of Windows 95 work for you.
To my Mom, Phyllis Nielsen, who patiently tolerates so many family computer conversations.

About the Author

Janice A. Snyder is an independent consultant and freelance writer, specializing in microcomputer desktop applications and Web page authoring. Prior to becoming a consultant, Jan was the director of the Administrative Computer Center at Indiana Wesleyan University. In the past year, she has contributed to Que books about Windows applications, including *Special Edition Using Microsoft Office 97* and *Special Edition Using Microsoft Office Professional for Windows 95*. Jan also has coauthored or edited many other books for Que Corporation, including books on MS Office, Word, Excel, PowerPoint, Access, dBASE, Quicken, QuickBooks, WinFax Pro, WordPerfect, Quattro Pro, and Internet applications. Jan can be reached by e-mail at **jan.snyder@mci2000.com**.

Acknowledgments

Thanks to Angie Wethington and Dana Coe at Que for their guidance on this book even through the changing guidelines and other miscellaneous obstacles, such as multiple versions of Windows 95.

Karen Cooper and Sheldon Dunn provided their excellent writing skills to keep the project on schedule. I thank God for them and appreciate their diligence and timely efforts.

Thanks also to Keith Underdahl for his superb technical editing to ensure the accuracy of this work, and to Sarah Rudy and the production team at Que.

To my husband, Alan, I am grateful for encouragement to keep working on this project. Now he owes me a vacation.

We'd Like to Hear from You!

As part of our continuing effort to produce books of the highest possible quality, Que would like to hear your comments. To stay competitive, we *really* want you, as a computer book reader and user, to let us know what you like or dislike most about this book or other Que products.

You can mail comments, ideas, or suggestions for improving future editions to the address below, or send us a fax at (317) 581-4663. For the online-inclined, Macmillan Computer Publishing has a forum on CompuServe (type **GO QUEBOOKS** at any prompt) through which our staff and authors are available for questions and comments. The address of our Internet site is **http://www.quecorp.com** (World Wide Web).

In addition to exploring our forum, please feel free to contact me personally to discuss your opinions of this book: I'm **73451,1220** on CompuServe, and **dcoe@que.mcp.com** on the Internet.

Thanks in advance—your comments will help us to continue publishing the best books available on computer topics in today's market.

Dana Coe
Product Development Specialist
Que Corporation
201 W. 103rd Street
Indianapolis, Indiana 46290
USA

NOTE Although we cannot provide general technical support, we're happy to help you resolve problems you encounter related to our books, disks, or other products. If you need such assistance, please contact our Tech Support department at 800-545-5914 ext. 3833.

To order other Que or Macmillan Computer Publishing books or products, please call our Customer Service department at 800-835-3202 ext. 666. ▪

Table of Contents

Introduction

The *Windows 95 Quick Reference* is one book in a series of
comprehensive, task-oriented references that details how to
use the features and functionality of Windows 95. Compiled for
the intermediate to advanced user who wants a concise, comprehensive reference, the *Windows 95 Quick Reference* is
loaded with detailed instructions outlining important tasks you
need to get the most from Windows 95.

The *Windows 95 Quick Reference* presents the tasks most often
sought by users of Windows 95. The book also includes a comprehensive glossary with many terms and definitions that refer
to the newest features in the Windows 95 product offering
from Microsoft.

New Ways of Working

Que's Quick References help the reader cover the most
ground with the least amount of hassle, and in a minimum of
time. Tasks include steps that the reader can complete, usually
with no more than five steps to any task.

The goal of the authors is to help you get your work done in
the least amount of time, with a minimum of reading. The
authors know that your time is valuable to you. You may not
need to use some of the included tasks very often, but when
you do, you want to look it up quickly and get back to work.
That's why each task in this book is written with economy in
mind. The reader should be able to recognize a need, take this
book off the shelf and complete a task within minutes, then put
the book back on the shelf for future reference. It just doesn't
get any faster or easier.

Expanded Coverage

Unlike other low-cost references, Que's *Windows 95 Quick Reference* covers every major functional subset of Windows 95. More importantly, each subset is covered separately, in its own dedicated section in this book. You can be confident that this book covers a lot of ground. The *Windows 95 Quick Reference* even includes "Networking" and "Multimedia" sections.

Who Should Read This Book?

The *Windows 95 Quick Reference* is written for casual to advanced computer users who need a fast reference to Windows 95 tasks and features. It is an ideal companion to Que's *Special Edition Using Microsoft Windows 95*. The Quick Reference size makes it ideal for travel.

If you are upgrading from Windows 3.11, you will find this reference useful for finding new features and looking up new ways of getting a job done. If you are migrating from another operating system, this Quick Reference may be the right amount of instruction you need to transfer your know-how investment to new products.

As a reference, this book is not intended to tutor learners. If you are just starting to use Windows 95 for the first time, or are a very casual user, you may want to consider Que's *Using Microsoft Windows 95* or *The Complete Idiot's Guide to Microsoft Windows 95* as a book to get you up to speed. For a beginner or very casual task reference, check out Que's *Easy Microsoft Windows 95*. If you want the most complete reference as well as tutorial and foundation information, then you need Que's *Special Edition Using Microsoft Windows 95*. This *Windows 95 Quick Reference* makes an ideal companion to the comprehensive Special Edition.

Features of This Book

If you take a moment to glance over the table of contents, you'll note that each logical part of the Windows 95 product has its own dedicated section in this book. Topics are organized into working groups under each logical part of Windows 95, with related tasks sorted under each topic in alphabetical order. In some cases, tasks have been specially sorted by the authors when task grouping, sequencing, or relationships indicate the order.

Content Tuned to Your Needs

You can't be expected to know everything, and yet, you don't have to be told everything in minute detail either. That's why the Quick Reference authors have been given wide latitude in determining what extra information you might find valuable to complete a task. By tuning the presentation to your needs, you can spend less time sifting through background information or cross-referencing related information just to be sure you're using a task appropriately. For example, the authors often indicate which conditions must exist in order to complete a task. The authors explain why one task is better to use over another—all in very succinct text. Where it is obvious to you what conditions must exist or which task is best, you won't be slowed by text telling you what you already know.

Expert Advice

Our expert authors know when a specific task is appropriate and when that task should be avoided. For example, there is no point in making a bulleted list if only one list item exists. This book tells you when a task is in order, and when you should avoid using a task when it's out of context or is not appropriate. This expertise of the authors transfers directly to your work.

Navigation and Steps

Author expertise can also help keep tasks simple by including or eliminating steps that guide you to where you enter information or perform an action. Tasks in this book that detail how to get where you're going do so because the authors believe that getting there is confusing for the reader.

In other cases, where your starting point is not relevant or where you are likely to know where a menu or dialog box is located, the authors keep it simple by not adding the navigational detail. The same assumptions apply where individual actions can be compounded into a step. Beginners often need "baby steps" to avoid confusion. The need for such care soon passes for most, and the user is better able to work with a step that is a logical group of actions. The result is a more readable set of steps.

The authors have limited the length of commands and steps to just the words you need to read to complete each task in a minimum of time. Intermediate users of Windows-based applications rarely need to be told when to click the OK button!

Expert Mentoring

You also get background information, when appropriate, to the topic or task. Tasks are often introduced so that your understanding of the real purpose of the task is clarified. Although mentoring is best done through the full *Special Edition Using* series, there are times when a little mentoring before a task greatly enhances the understanding of that task or feature. The authors keep this in mind while using their extensive user experience to determine when to provide that reinforcing conceptual information.

A Comprehensive Glossary

With the Internet awareness of the Microsoft Windows 95 product comes a lot of jargon that will be new to you. This book has a glossary of terms specific to who you are and what you're doing. These terms are contained in various sections of the book as italicized words. Look them up as you go along, or scan for any terms that you may not be familiar with. Ever wonder what a *property* is? You don't have to complete a task to find out. You can check out such terms or definitions in the glossary!

Task Reference

This Quick Reference is divided into sections, all dedicated to Windows 95 operational areas. In each section, you will find an alphabetical listing of topics that are detailed with tasks.

To find all tasks that cover printing, for example, find the task topic "Printing," then turn to the tasks that cover activities in that topic area. Tasks are sorted in alphabetical order unless there is special value in completing multiple tasks in order.

When a prerequisite task must be read to understand the task you are reading, a cross-reference will let you know: (See "WordPad: Editing a Document" and "Closing a Document: Saving" before you complete this task.) When other tasks may be more useful, or may be used instead of the task you are viewing, a cross-reference will let you know where to find it: (See also "Files and Folders: Viewing in Explorer" in the "Disk and File Management" part of this book.) And when other related tasks may be useful after completing a task, a cross-reference at the end of the task will direct you to their location: (See also "Sharing: Using Object Linking and Embedding (OLE).")

Conventions Used in This Book

This book is based on Microsoft Windows 95, version 4.00.950 A. If your version of Windows 95 is different, your steps for some tasks will vary. To check your version of Windows, right-click the My Computer icon, choose Properties, and look at the System entry on the General page. In most cases, this book provides a Note to describe an alternate method you can use if you are using version 4.00.950b of Windows 95.

Where the steps differ, you'll find the following Note, sometimes followed by another Note with the alternate version B steps in paragraph form.

NOTE These steps are based on Microsoft Windows 95, version 4.00.950 A. If your version of Windows 95 is different, your steps for this task will vary. To check your version of Windows, right-click the My Computer icon, choose Properties, and look at the System entry on the General page. ■

This book uses certain conventions in order to guide you through the various tasks. Special typefaces in this Quick Reference include the following.

Type	Meaning
italics	Terms or phrases that may be found in the Glossary; variables.
underline	Shortcut key combinations for menu commands and dialog box options that appear underlined on-screen.
boldface	Information you are asked to type.
computer type	Direct quotations of words that appear on-screen or in a figure.

When a direction is given to "click," this means click the left side of the mouse control for those mice with alternate buttons. When it is necessary for the right or alternate side of the mouse to be used, the direction "right-click" will be given.

In most cases, keys are represented as they appear on the keyboard. The arrow keys are usually represented by name (for example, the *up-arrow key*). The Print Screen key is abbreviated PrtSc; Page Up is PgUp; Insert is Ins; and so on. On your keyboard, these key names may be spelled out or abbreviated differently.

When two keys appear together with a plus sign, such as Shift+Ins, press and hold the first key as you press the second key. When two keys appear together without a plus sign, such as End, Home, press and release the first key before you press the second key.

Various toolbar buttons, such as the one shown here, are used throughout the steps and are identified with a visual icon next to the appropriate step. These icons resemble the on-screen toolbar buttons and make it easier for you to find them quickly.

Many tasks include Warnings, Cautions, Notes, Tips, and Troubleshootings. These are described in-depth in the following paragraphs.

The authors have gone to great lengths to protect you from disaster, often warning you of impending, often irreversible danger before you get in over your head. Warnings are just one way this Quick Reference will inform you when you need to know.

> **WARNING**   Formatting a previously formatted disk will destroy any files previously stored on the disk. Be sure the floppy doesn't contain anything you need before you format it.

The completion of some tasks may change the way Windows 95 works in the future. Cautions inform the reader about unforeseen events that may not occur as expected. Cautions are not as severe as Warnings, but you will want to read cautionary information.

> **CAUTION**   Although Windows 95 can automatically truncate long file names, older versions of Windows or DOS may not be able to use files with long names. So, if you exchange files with someone running older operating systems, you will need to stick to the previous 8.3 naming convention.

Notes often advise and direct you while you complete a task. Expect to find useful guidance while you complete tasks.

NOTE   The hard disk you specify for virtual memory must have at least as much free space as the maximum amount of virtual memory you set. ▨

Tips offer expert input from those who really know the software. Tips often include time-saving solutions and ways to shortcut your way to success. If you're looking for a shortcut, tips are where you'll find them!

TIP You should close all applications and stop working on the system while the Defragment utility is running. *Defragmenting* your drive can take a while, especially if you have a large hard drive or your hard drive is especially fragmented. So you might want to start the utility and let it run while you are at lunch.

Troubleshootings state problems that you are likely to encounter and how to solve them. These are often the problems that the expert authors have faced, or common problems that other users experience. Troubleshootings give the quickest and most appropriate way of addressing the stated problem.

TROUBLESHOOTING **When I copy text with drag and drop, the original text is deleted.** You used the move feature instead of copying. Hold down the Ctrl key before dragging. Release the mouse button first and then release the Ctrl key.

Related Books

No one book can cover all of the needs of every user. Que offers a complete line of Windows 95-related titles. *Special Edition Using Microsoft Windows 95* is the most complete tu-torial and reference volume available for Windows 95, and answers end-user questions with clear, concise, and comprehensive authority. Ask your bookseller for the availability of other Que titles.

Windows 95 Basics

This part of the book introduces you to the basic screen elements in Windows 95. With a few guidelines, the Windows 95 desktop is easy to navigate. You have desktop icons, a taskbar, and a Start menu to take you anywhere you need to go on your system.

Even if you are an experienced Windows user, you may learn a few tips about the new ways to work in Windows 95. Learn how to manage windows on the desktop, switch between applications using the taskbar, and find your way around on the Start menu.

You also learn how to start and exit Windows 95. Just in case you need it, we touch on how to install, update, and remove Windows 95.

 This book is based on Microsoft Windows 95, version 4.00.950 A. If your version of Windows 95 is different, your steps for some tasks will vary. To check your version of Windows, right-click the My Computer icon, choose Properties, and look at the System entry on the General page. In most cases, this book provides a Note to describe an alternate method you can use if you are using version 4.00.950b of Windows 95.

Desktop: Arranging Icons

Desktop shortcut icons give you easy access to your programs, especially when you arrange them in a way that works best for you. You can arrange the icons using drag-and-drop, or choose commands to sort them in an order that you want.

Steps

1. Right-click a blank area of the desktop.
2. In the shortcut menu, point to Arrange Icons and then choose from the cascading menu items shown in the following table.

Command	Action
By Name	Sort items alphabetically by file name.
By Type	Sort items by file type. Files with the same extension are grouped together.
By Size	Sort items by file size, from smallest to largest.
By Date	Sort items by date, from oldest to the most recent.
Auto Arrange	Toggle this choice on—indicated by a check mark—or off to automatically arrange icons at the left side of the desktop. When you move an icon, it will snap into a new position, moving the other icons to make room.

TIP   If you want to simply realign icons, not change their order, choose the Line Up Icons command on the desktop shortcut menu or on a window's View menu. This command does nothing if the Auto Arrange option is toggled on, because auto arranging keeps the icons aligned automatically. Toggle Auto Arrange off if you want to arrange your icons spread all over the desktop, not crowded to the left side. Then use the Line Up Icons command to line them up on the imaginary grid in their same general vicinity.

NOTE   The same icon arrangement commands are available within Windows. Within Explorer, for example, you can choose

View, Arrange Icons, then select from the same commands shown in the previous table. Some windows offer fewer choices or window-specific choices. The My Computer window, for example, allows you to arrange icons by Drive Letter or by Free Space. ■

Desktop: Closing a Window

After you have finished using a window or *application*, you can leave the window open or close it. Your desktop could become very cluttered if you open many windows, however; and a large number of open applications could adversely affect system performance. For these reasons, you should close windows when you are finished using them.

Steps

1. Click the icon in the window's upper-left corner.
2. Choose Close on the Control menu.

You also can close a window by any of the following methods.

■ Click the Close button in the window's upper-right corner.

■ Double-click the icon in the window's upper-left corner.

■ Open the File menu (if the application has one) and choose Close or Exit (if the application has these commands).

■ Right-click the window's taskbar button. Choose Close.

■ Press Alt+F4.

> **CAUTION**   If you attempt to close an application window without saving a document, the application will warn you and give you an opportunity to save the document. (See also "Closing a Document: Without Saving" in the "Applications and Accessories" part of this book.) You must choose to save or not save the document before the application window will close.

Desktop: Minimizing and Maximizing Windows

You can minimize or maximize a window. Within an application, minimizing a document window reduces the document to a button at the lower edge of the application window. Maximizing a document window enlarges the document to the full size of the application window, which may or may not be full-screen size.

Steps

1. Click the icon in the window's upper-left corner.

2. On the Control menu, choose Minimize to minimize the window, or choose Maximize to maximize the window.

You also can minimize or maximize a window using the following methods.

- Click the Minimize button or the Maximize button in the window's upper-right corner.

- Right-click the taskbar button that represents the window. Choose Minimize to minimize the window, or choose Maximize to maximize the window.

TIP To minimize all windows on the desktop, right-click the taskbar (on a blank part) and then choose Minimize All Windows. To restore all windows, right-click the taskbar and choose Undo Minimize All.

(See also "Desktop: Restoring a Minimized or Maximized Window" to restore a window to its previous size.)

Desktop: Moving Windows

Often, you will want to move a window out of the way so you can access a desktop icon or view the contents of another window. The easiest way to move a window on the desktop is to use *drag-and-drop*.

Steps

1. Position the mouse pointer on the title bar of the window.

2. Hold down the left mouse button.

3. Drag the item to the desired position.

4. Release the mouse button.

You can also use the keyboard to move a window. Press Alt+spacebar to open the Control menu icon in the upper-left corner of the window. The window is surrounded by a gray border. Choose <u>M</u>ove and then use the keyboard arrow keys to position the window. Press Enter to complete the move.

Desktop: Opening a Window or Application

Almost every activity in Windows 95 requires opening a window. While you probably know at least two ways to open a window or application, maybe you haven't tried all of the available methods.

Steps

1. Click the Start button.

2. Click a command, menu, folder, or document.

The following are some of the other ways to open a window or application.

- Double-click an icon on the desktop.

- From Explorer, double-click an application or document icon.

- From My Computer, double-click an application or document icon.

- Click an icon on a separate program's shortcut bar, such as the Microsoft Office Shortcut Bar.

TIP   If you open a document file or a document's shortcut icon, the document's accompanying application opens automatically.

Desktop: Resizing Windows

If your window has scroll bars, then you can possibly enlarge the window to see more of its contents without scrolling. For example, maybe you can't see all of the icons on your Control

Panel window unless you scroll. If you resize the window to enlarge it, all icons will be visible and the scroll bars disappear.

Steps

1. Position the mouse pointer on any corner or side of the window. The pointer changes to a double-headed arrow.

2. Hold down the left mouse button.

3. Drag the item to the desired size. Drag toward the window to reduce the size; drag away from the window to enlarge it. An outline shows the proposed size.

4. Release the mouse button.

You can use the keyboard to size a window. Press Alt+spacebar to open the Control menu icon in the upper-left corner of the window. Choose Size and then use the keyboard arrow keys to size the window. Press Enter to quit sizing the window.

Desktop: Restoring a Minimized or Maximized Window

When you minimize a window, it becomes a button on the taskbar. To restore it (return it to window size), just click the taskbar button that represents the window. To restore a minimized document within an application, click its minimized button in the application window.

When you maximize a window, it takes up the full screen or the full size of its application window if it is a document. To restore a maximized window, use the following steps.

Steps

1. Click the icon in the window's upper-left corner to open the Control menu.

2. Choose Restore to return the window to its previous size.

The following are additional methods for restoring a maximized window.

■ Click the Restore button in the window's upper-right corner.

■ Right-click the taskbar button that represents the window. Choose <u>R</u>estore.

(See also "Desktop: Minimizing and Maximizing Windows.")

Desktop: Selecting a Window

Although you may have multiple applications running, with windows all over your desktop, only one window is active at a time. If you want to work in a window, it must be selected.

You can see which window is currently active because its title bar is a different color—usually brighter or darker, while the other title bars become more faded. (This may not be true if you have customized the window colors.) If windows overlap, the active one is on top. Also, the active window's taskbar button appears lighter and looks like it is pressed in.

You can select a window, and therefore switch applications, by using the following steps.

Steps

1. Locate the window's button in the taskbar.
2. Click the window's taskbar button. This is the best method if some of the open windows are maximized, covering the view of any other windows.

Use any of the following additional methods for selecting a window.

■ Click the window's title bar.

■ Click almost any other part of the window that is visible and won't perform an undesired action (such as closing the window).

■ Hold down Alt and then press Tab repeatedly until the application window you want is selected. Then release the Alt key.

WINDOWS 95 BASICS

TIP Make all windows selectable by cascading or tiling them. Right-click a blank part of the taskbar and choose Cascade, Tile Horizontally, or Tile Vertically. (See also "Taskbar: Using the Taskbar Menu" in the "Customizing Windows 95" part of this book.)

(See also "Switching: Between Applications" in the "Applications and Accessories" part of this book.)

Exiting: Windows 95

When you finish running Windows applications and want to turn off the computer, you must first correctly exit Windows. Some data is stored in memory and is not written to the hard disk until you use the Shut Down command.

> **CAUTION** Don't ever turn your computer off without exiting Windows. You could lose data. Wait for the message saying it is safe to turn your computer off.

Steps

1. Save documents and other data in applications that are open; and exit all applications, including DOS applications.

2. Choose Start, Shut Down. The Shut Down Windows dialog box appears with the following options (which may vary depending on your configuration):

   *Shut Down the Computer?

   *Restart the Computer?

   *Restart the Computer in MS-DOS Mode?

   *Close All Programs and Log on as a Different User?

3. Choose Shut Down the Computer.

4. Click Yes.

5. Turn off your computer when you see the message that says it is safe to do so.

NOTE Perhaps you have changed hardware configurations or other Windows settings that present a window telling you that you must restart your computer for the changes to take effect. If you deferred restarting the computer when prompted, you can restart the computer (reboot) without shutting down completely. Choose the Restart the Computer? option in the Shut Down Windows dialog box. ▪

TIP To restart Windows without restarting the computer, hold down the Shift key when you choose Restart the Computer?

Help: In Dialog Boxes

You can get quick help right where you need it without getting into extensive explanations. In most Windows applications, a Help button appears at the top-right corner of dialog boxes and windows. The Help button looks like a question mark.

Steps

1. Open any dialog box and click its Help button. A question mark attaches to the pointer.

2. Click the *control* that you want information about. For example, click a list box or option button. A description box appears.

3. Click the left mouse button to close the description box.

TIP Access a Help description box in another way that may be available even when there is no Help button. Right-click an object or control. Click the What's This box that pops up. A description appears.

If you need more help than the description boxes supply, use the Help menu to look for the subject. (See also "Help: On the Desktop.")

Help: In Windows

Many windows, including most application windows, have a
Help menu. The command you choose on the menu varies
with applications, so these steps refer to windows in Windows.

Steps

1. Open a window. For this example, open the My Computer window by double-clicking the My Computer icon
   on the desktop.

2. Choose Help, Help Topics. The Help Topics dialog box
   appears.

3. Choose a tab and follow the instructions on the page.

4. Click the Close button to close the Help Topics dialog
   box or a Help window.

(See also "Help: On the Desktop" for more details.)

Help: On the Desktop

Help for Windows topics is available from the Start menu.
If you can't remember how to perform a task in Windows,
you can start here.

Steps

1. Choose Start, Help. The Help Topics dialog box is
   displayed.

2. Choose from the following tabs:

   *Contents.   A topical list that includes a tour, introduc-
   tion, how to…, tips and tricks, and troubleshooting. This
   is a good place to start if you don't know quite what to
   look up.

   *Index.   Locate help by typing the first few letters of the
   word you are looking for. The index locates topics
   related to what you type, searching only its list of topics.

   *Find.   Locates items by full text search of the Help
   files, not just the topic titles. The first time you use Find

in an application, the Setup Wizard builds a database of the Help text.

3. Follow the instructions on the page to locate a Help topic. Select a topic and then choose Display, or double-click the topic. Help appears in another window and the Help Topics dialog box closes.

4. Click the Close button when you are finished with the Help window.

TIP Print a topic from a Help window by choosing Options, Print Topic.

Within a Help window there are several buttons; these are described in the following table.

Using the Help Window

Button	Action
Help Topics	Redisplay the Help Topics window.
Back	Return to the previous topic.
Options	Display commands for using Help topics: Annotate, Copy, Print Topic, Font, Keep Help on Top, and Use System Colors.
Related Topics	Display list of related Help topics. This button, when present, is usually found at the end of the Help text.

NOTE Besides getting help within Windows or by using a book like this one, you can find support online through the Microsoft Network and various computer bulletin board forums. CompuServe gives you access to forums and the Microsoft Knowledge Base.

On the Internet, access Microsoft's World Wide Web site at **http://ww.microsoft.com**. You will find a wealth of troubleshooting information about Windows and other Microsoft applications.

WINDOWS 95 BASICS

Navigating: The Start Menu

The Start menu is a straightforward tool for starting applications. Your desktop may be obscured with open windows. Instead of moving or minimizing windows to access a desktop shortcut icon, you can always use the Start menu to open your application and perform almost every other task in Windows 95.

Steps

1. Click the Start button. The Start menu pops up.
2. Move the pointer along the menu. Submenus pop up for some of the items: Find, Settings, Documents, and Programs.
3. To move to a submenu item, point to the Start menu item, and then move the pointer either left or right to the submenu. Move the pointer up or down within the submenu.
4. When the application, document, or command you want is highlighted, click to select it.

TIP   If you have a newer keyboard, it may have built-in Windows keys. Look between the Ctrl and Alt keys. If you see a key with the Windows logo, press it to open the Start menu. You may also have a key with an icon that looks like a menu. Press it to open a shortcut menu related to the cursor's position on-screen.

TROUBLESHOOTING   **Where is File Manager? I want to see my files.** Windows 95 does not have the File Manager you used in Windows 3.x, but gives you Explorer to manage your files. You can find Windows Explorer on the Start, Programs menu. (See also "Files and Folders: Viewing in Explorer" in the "Disk and File Management" part of this book.)

What happened to all of my old Windows 3.1 program groups? When you upgraded from Windows 3.1, Windows 95 put your program groups on the Start, Programs menu as folders. You can move or copy these groups to the desktop, represented by a folder icon. (See also "Shortcuts: Creating on Desktop" in the "Applications and Accessories" part of this book.)

Setup: Installing Windows 95

If you purchased a new computer in the past year, it is likely that Windows 95 was already installed for you. Therefore, this section focuses on installation from a working Windows 3.x system.

Minimum system requirements as specified by Microsoft for installing Windows 95 are:

- 486/25 MHz-based system
- 8M of memory (RAM)
- 40M of available hard disk space
- Microsoft Mouse or compatible pointing device
- VGA or higher resolution display

Steps

1. Start Windows 3.x. Put the CD-ROM or the first disk in the drive. In Program Manager, choose File, Run and enter **a:\setup** in the Command Line box. (Substitute a different drive letter for a: if necessary.) The Setup program starts.

2. Continue through the Setup program, answering prompts as required. You will be asked to accept the license agreement, save system files, choose a setup option, provide your name, enter the serial number from your Windows 95 disk/CD, select hardware to configure, install online services, and create a Startup disk.

3. Windows 95 files are copied to your system. Choose Finish. Your system reboots and then takes several more minutes to complete configuring Windows 95.

You can decide not to install some features of Windows 95 initially. You can add Windows Setup applications later in the Add/Remove Programs Properties sheet.

> **CAUTION** After you install the Windows 95 upgrade version, you should retain your old Windows 3.x disks even if you do not intend to use them again. You will need the first Windows 3.x disk if you install the Windows 95 upgrade version on a new or reformatted hard drive.

Refer to Que's *Windows 95 Installation and Configuration Handbook* for more details on installing and configuring Windows 95.

Updating Your Copy of Windows 95

Windows 95 was not updated in a full 1996 version. Instead, upgrades have been released as Service Packs. To order a copy of the latest Service Pack, call 800-360-7561 and request the latest Windows 95 Service Pack. There is a charge of $14.95, plus $5.00 shipping and handling, plus tax. Or, download the Service Pack free on online services or the Internet. The Internet location is: **http://www.microsoft.com/windows95**. Look for the Free Software and Product Update links to find the Service Pack.

> **CAUTION** Service Pack 1 was intended for earlier versions of Windows 95, up to 4.00.950 A. If you are using the 4.00.950b version of Windows 95, you should not install Service Pack 1. The 4.00.950b version includes the updates from Service Pack 1. To check your version of Windows, right-click the My Computer icon, choose Properties, and look at the System entry on the General page.

 TIP You should check files you download from the Internet by running a virus-checking program.

Setup: Removing Windows 95

If you have DOS and Windows 3.x on your computer and you selected the option to save your old Windows 3.x and DOS system files during Windows 95 setup, then you can remove all traces of Windows 95 to return to your Windows 3.x installation.

One way to know if you can safely remove Windows 95 is to see if Windows 95 is on the list of files that can be removed in the Install/Uninstall page of the Add/Remove Programs Properties sheet (accessed within the Control Panel). If Windows 95 is on the list, then you can remove it.

Steps

1. If you are running disk compression in Windows 95, uncompress the hard drive. You may need to delete some files to have space to uncompress the drive.

2. Choose Start, Settings, Control Panel. Double-click the Add/Remove Programs icon. Click the Install/ Uninstall tab.

3. Select Windows 95 in the list box and then click Add/ Remove. A warning box informs you that you are about to remove Windows 95 and restore your previous versions of Windows and MS-DOS.

4. Click Yes to remove Windows 95. Click No if you changed your mind and don't want to remove Windows 95.

CAUTION If you have installed any applications since installing Windows 95, you will probably have to reconfigure or reinstall them to work with Windows 3.1. Some applications designed to work with Windows 95, such as Microsoft Office 95, will not run in Windows 3.1.

NOTE If you can't boot into Windows 95 and you want to uninstall it, boot from the startup disk you created during setup. At the A: prompt, type **uninstall**. After Windows 95 is removed, you may still have to remove some long file names in Windows 3.x File Manager. ▦

For steps to uncompress a compressed drive, see "DriveSpace: Returning to Normal" in the "Disk and File Management" part of this book.

Starting: Windows 95

After installing Windows 95, you start Windows by turning on your computer. Although you will see drivers load in a DOS-like text screen, a normal Windows 95 startup goes on to display the desktop.

If your installation of Windows has multiple configurations, such as for a laptop and desktop version, a text screen displays, allowing you to choose the configuration before Windows starts. If you have set up Windows for multiple users, you see a login sheet in which you type your password. Windows loads the configuration for the logged-in user.

Steps

1. Turn on the computer.
2. Wait for drivers to load, memory check, and so on.
3. If multiple configurations are presented, choose one.
4. If a login sheet is presented, log in with password. Windows 95 displays the desktop with icons, taskbar, and Start menus, as shown in Figure 1.

The desktop is the background on which you work in Windows 95. Shortcut icons allow you to start programs quickly when you double-click them. The Start button opens the Start menu, which has submenus leading to many other folders and applications. The taskbar displays buttons for your open applications and windows. Windows open on the desktop and can be moved around and resized.

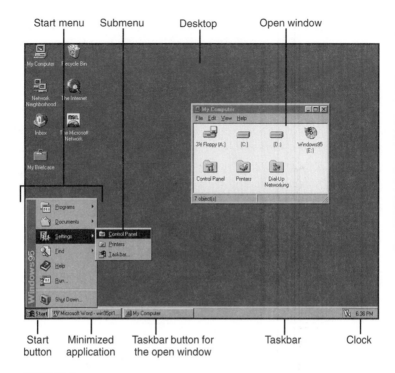

FIGURE 1

Windows 95 displays the desktop on startup. Here, an application (minimized) and window have been opened.

Note in Figure 1 that the icon for My Computer remains on the desktop even though its window is currently open. It also has a button on the taskbar used for selecting it if it is covered by another window.

Applications and Accessories

Windows 95 provides a variety of accessory programs to increase your productivity, especially when used with other *applications*. Most of these accessory programs are installed with Windows 95 or can be added later, and are accessed on the Accessories submenu, which is located on the Programs menu. Examples of accessories described in this part of the book are Calculator, Character Map, Clipboard Viewer, Notepad, Paint, and WordPad. Other accessories are described in other parts of this book.

Many of the skills used in managing applications are common to most Windows applications. Opening, closing, and saving documents will entail the same basic procedure and have the same Windows 95 "look" in applications designed for Windows 95. These common tasks are described in this section. In Windows 95, there is often more than one way to perform a task such as starting a program. In some cases, this book describes multiple methods, but often the focus will be on the easiest way to accomplish the task, frequently involving use of the mouse and toolbars.

Calculator: Copying Numbers

The Windows Calculator accessory looks and operates much like a calculator you keep in your desk drawer. An advantage to using the Windows Calculator, however, is that you can copy numbers between the Calculator and other applications. Copying numbers helps you avoid mistakes created by retyping the entries or results.

Steps

1. Open the Calculator by choosing Start, Programs, Accessories, Calculator.

2. Using the mouse or keyboard numeric keypad, enter numbers and operators. End by pressing the = button to display the result of the calculation in the Calculator display window.

3. Choose Edit, Copy in the Calculator menu bar.

4. Position the *insertion point* in the other application where you want to place the calculated number.

5. In the application, choose Edit, Paste.

TIP   Copy a number from an application to the Calculator display window by selecting the number and choosing Edit, Copy in the application. Then choose Edit, Paste in Calculator.

TROUBLESHOOTING   **When I type numbers on the keyboard, the numbers are not displayed in the Calculator window.** If you are using the numeric keypad (recommended) at the right side of the keyboard, you must press the Num Lock key before typing numbers.

Calculator: Scientific

The Scientific Calculator is an extension of the Calculator, adding many advanced functions. You can perform statistical calculations, such as standard deviations and averages, and scientific functions such as sines, cosines, tangents, powers, and logarithms.

Steps

1. Open the Calculator by choosing Start, Programs, Accessories, Calculator.

2. Choose View, Scientific in the Calculator menu bar.

3. Select a number system:

   *Hex = hexadecimal

   *Dec = decimal (the default)

*Oct = octal

*Bin = binary

4. Enter numbers and operators as needed for your calculation.

5. Click the = button to display the result.

You can return to the Standard Calculator by choosing <u>V</u>iew, Standard in the Scientific Calculator menu bar.

TIP   For help on the use of a Calculator button, right-click the button and then click the <u>W</u>hat's This? command that pops up. For more information on the use of advanced functions, review Calculator's <u>H</u>elp menu, <u>H</u>elp Topics.

NOTE   Statistical calculations require use of the Statistical box for entry of data. In the Scientific Calculator, click Sta, and then enter each number, clicking Dat after each number. After all data for the calculation is entered, click Sta and then click the statistical function button you want. ■

Character Map: Inserting Symbols

The Character Map accessory is used to insert special symbols and *ANSI characters* into a document. For example, to insert the registered trademark symbol, you can copy it from the Character Map and then insert it into your document. Some Windows programs, such as Microsoft Word, have a built-in capability to select such symbols (try <u>I</u>nsert, <u>S</u>ymbol in Word). Use the Character Map with applications that do not provide this function.

If the Character Map is not installed on your computer, refer to "Windows Components: Adding and Removing" in the "Customizing Windows 95" part of this book.

Steps

1. Open Character Map by choosing Start, <u>P</u>rograms, Accessories, Character Map.

2. In the <u>F</u>ont drop-down list, choose the font you want to use.

APPLICATIONS AND ACCESSORIES

3. Select a character by double-clicking it, which places it in the Characters to Copy box. Select additional characters by double-clicking them.

4. Click the Copy button, which places the selected characters on the Clipboard.

5. Position the insertion point in the application where you want to copy the characters, and then choose Edit, Paste.

   If the application you are copying characters to has a Paste button, you can click it instead of choosing Edit, Paste.

When you are finished with the Character Map accessory, click its Close button.

 TIP To view an enlarged image of a character before selecting it, click and hold down the mouse button on the character. You can use the arrow keys to move the selection box around to view an enlarged image of each character.

Clipboard: Copying Data

When you cut or copy and then paste information within an application or between applications, Windows uses the Clipboard to store the data. You don't normally see the Clipboard—it is a memory location. Its contents become evident when you paste the data.

Steps

1. Select the text or data to highlight it.

 2. Click the Copy button (to copy) or the Cut button (to move).

 3. Place the insertion point where you want to paste the data.

 4. Click the Paste button.

Data you cut or copy to the Clipboard stays there even after you paste it. You can paste the same Clipboard data repeatedly if needed. But the next time you cut or copy other data, it replaces the current contents of the Clipboard.

Clipboard: Viewing

What if you have copied or cut data and want to see the current contents of the Windows Clipboard? Windows 95 includes a Clipboard Viewer utility that allows you to view and save the contents of the Clipboard.

Steps

1. Open Clipboard Viewer by choosing Start, Programs, Accessories, Clipboard Viewer.

   The contents of the Clipboard appear in the Clipboard Viewer window.

2. If you want to save the Clipboard data, choose File, Save As, and then save it with the .CLP extension.

3. Click the Clipboard Viewer window Close button to close the Clipboard.

 TIP   Because the Clipboard contents reside in your computer's memory, you can free some memory by clearing the Clipboard. In the Clipboard Viewer window, choose Edit, Delete or press the Delete key. You are prompted to clear the contents of the Clipboard. Click Yes to clear the Clipboard.

NOTE   The Clipboard Viewer is not installed during a Typical setup of Windows 95. You must choose it from the Accessories in the Custom setup. To add it after Windows 95 is installed, see the task "Windows Components: Adding and Removing" in the "Customizing Windows 95" part of this book. ▪

 TIP   If you saved the contents of the Clipboard to a .CLP file, you can retrieve the contents by opening the Clipboard Viewer and then choosing File, Open. The saved file appears in the Clipboard Viewer window, and the contents are available for pasting in applications.

Clock: Taskbar

 The Windows 95 clock is displayed on the taskbar. When you place the mouse pointer on the clock, the date is displayed. If you need to change the date or time or correct the time zone, display the properties sheet. The Date/Time properties are accessible from the Date/Time icon in the Control Panel, or directly from the taskbar.

Steps

1. Double-click the time on the taskbar.

2. On the Date & Time properties page, select any of the Date options you want to change: month, year, or day. Choose the correct setting.

3. Select any part of the Time display you want to change: hour, minute, second, AM/PM. Use the arrows to adjust to the correct setting.

4. If the Current Time Zone display is incorrect, choose the Time Zone page and select the correct time zone from the drop-down list. Choose OK to save the changes to the date, time, and time zone.

If the clock is not displayed on the taskbar, or if the clock is displayed and you want to hide it, you can change a taskbar setting to display or hide the clock. (See also "Taskbar: Changing Options" in the "Customizing Windows 95" part of this book.)

Closing a Document: Saving

When you have finished creating or making changes to a document—such as a word processing document or spreadsheet—you usually want to save the document to disk. Most programs designed for Windows 95 use similar commands and dialog boxes for saving and closing documents, as described here.

Steps

1. If the application has a Save button in a toolbar, click it. Or choose File, Save.

If the document has already been named and saved previously, it is resaved, but remains open. If the document has not previously been saved, the Save As dialog box appears.

2. If the Save As dialog box appears, choose a drive and folder in the Save In drop-down list. In the File Name text box, type a name for the document (or keep the name that appears in the text box). Choose Save.

3. To close the document, click the Close button in the upper-right corner of the document window.

   If you have not already saved the document, a message appears asking if you want to save the document. Choose Yes to save the document.

NOTE In some applications, there is a Close button for the document window that looks like an X, the same as the Close button for the application. If you intend to keep using the application, be sure to choose the document's Close button to close only the current document and not the application.

TIP Create a new version of an existing file by choosing File, Save As, and then specifying a new name for the file.

CAUTION If you save a file as a different type than the application in which it was created, you may lose some formatting changes and any other features not available in the application type you choose.

Closing a Document: Without Saving

Occasionally, you may make changes to a document and want to close the document without saving those changes.

Why Close Without Saving?

You may have rearranged or deleted text in the document and then regretted it. While many Windows programs allow you to

APPLICATIONS AND ACCESSORIES

undo actions, sometimes it is simpler to start over from the previously stored document.

You can close a new document without naming it, thus abandoning it without saving it. You also can close an existing (previously named) document without saving the changes you made since the last save—in this case, reverting to the existing document on disk.

Steps

1. Click the document's Close button (the X in the upper-right corner of the document window).

2. If you are prompted to save the document, choose <u>N</u>o.

   The document is closed without saving it. If it was previously saved, the former version remains on disk after closing.

Copying and Moving: Drag and Drop

With Windows applications that support *drag and drop*, you can move or copy items using the mouse instead of menu commands or toolbar buttons. Drag and drop is a shortcut to using the Copy, Cut, and Paste commands.

Steps

1. Open a Windows application, such as WordPad or Word, that supports drag and drop.

2. Select the text or object you want to copy or move.

3. With the mouse pointer on the selected text or object, click and hold down the left mouse button.

   In most applications, if you are copying—not only moving—you must also hold down the Ctrl key.

4. Move the mouse to drag the text or object to the new location. A gray vertical line indicates the exact location.

5. Release the mouse button (and the Ctrl key) to drop the copied or moved text or object at the new location.

You can drag and drop text and objects between two documents by first displaying both documents on-screen. Drag and

drop between two applications to embed objects. (See also
"Sharing: Using Object Linking and Embedding (OLE).")

**TROUBLESHOOTING   When I copy text with drag and
drop, the original text is deleted.** You used the move feature
instead of copying. Hold down the Ctrl key before dragging.
Release the mouse button first and then release the Ctrl key.

**When I try to copy, the mouse pointer turns into a black circle
with a slash through it.** The black circle with a slash indicates
you can't copy to that area. Move the mouse completely into the
other document before releasing the mouse button.

Copying Between Applications: DOS to Windows

Windows 95 supports the following transfer of information
between DOS and Windows applications:

- Transfer text from DOS to Windows, from Windows to
  DOS, and between DOS applications by using the
  Clipboard.
- Transfer graphics from DOS to Windows applications by
  using the Clipboard.
- Copy text from the MS-DOS command prompt to the
  Clipboard.

Steps

1. Open the DOS application in a window and display the
   data you want to copy.

2. Click the Mark toolbar button. A blinking cursor appears
   in the DOS window, indicating that you are in marking
   mode.

3. Click and drag with the mouse to select the data you
   want to copy, and then release the mouse button.

4. Click the Copy button in the toolbar.

5. Switch to the Windows application, place the cursor
   where you want the data to be copied, and then click the
   Paste button in the toolbar of the Windows application.

NOTE Copying data from a Windows application to a DOS application is accomplished by copying the data in the Windows application, switching to the DOS application, and then choosing Edit, Paste from the Control menu of the DOS application. The DOS application must be running in a window, not full screen. If you do not see the toolbar in the DOS application, press Alt+Enter to restore the DOS application's window. ▧

(See also "Clipboard: Copying Data" and "Clipboard: Viewing.")

Installing: MS-DOS Applications

You can install MS-DOS applications by running the installation program for the application—if it has an installation program.

Steps

1. Start an MS-DOS session in Windows 95.

2. At the DOS prompt, enter the command to start the installation program and then press Enter. The command may be similar to **a:\install.exe**.

3. Follow directions for the installation program and then close the MS-DOS session.

(See also "MS-DOS Prompt: Controlling the Session" and "Starting Programs: MS-DOS Applications.")

NOTE If the MS-DOS application does not have an installation program, you can install it by creating a new folder and copying the files to it. Always look for a text file with more instructions, often named README.TXT or INSTALL.TXT, and read the file using WordPad or Notepad. (See also "WordPad: Creating or Opening a Document" or "Notepad: Using.") ▧

If your MS-DOS application can be run in a window, you will probably have to create your own Start menu item for the application. (See "Starting Programs: From Start Menu.")

NOTE   Usually when you install a DOS application, Windows creates a shortcut for it and places it in that application's folder. Use Explorer to copy the shortcut to the desktop. (See "Shortcuts: Creating on Desktop.") ■

Installing: Windows 3.1 Applications

In Windows 95 you can successfully install and run most Windows 3.1 applications. Typically, Windows 3.1 programs direct you to use File, Run in Program Manager or File Manager. In Windows 95, the Run command is found on the Start menu.

NOTE   For a current list of programs with known incompatibility problems with Windows 95, refer to the PROGRAMS.TXT file in the Windows folder. You also can check various online services for patches and information on workarounds. ■

Steps

1. Choose Start, Run.

2. In the Open box, type the command the program requires for installation, such as **a:\setup**.

3. Choose OK and then follow the application's setup instructions.

Windows 95 translates some actions of a Windows 3.1 application's Setup program into the Windows 95 equivalent. For example, Windows 95 converts Program Manager groups to Programs menu shortcuts on the Start menu. Running the Windows 3.1 application is much the same as running a Windows 95 application, except it will take on the Windows 95 look for the title bar and other window elements.

TIP   Another way to install the application is to open My Computer and then double-click the drive icon for the drive containing the installation disk. Locate the Setup program's icon and double-click it to install the application.

APPLICATIONS AND ACCESSORIES

> **CAUTION** If you created a dual-boot system by installing Windows 95 in a directory separate from Windows 3.1, adding Windows 3.1 applications to your Start menu isn't enough to successfully run them in Windows 95. You need to reinstall the application in Windows 95, specifying the same folder name.

Installing: Windows 95 Applications

Installing a Windows 95 application is as easy as running the application's Setup program; however, you can choose to run the Install Programs Wizard.

Steps

1. Choose Start, Settings, Control Panel to open the Control Panel window.

2. Double-click Add/Remove Programs.

3. In the Install/Uninstall page of the Add/Remove Programs properties sheet, choose Install.

4. Insert the program's disk or CD in the appropriate drive and choose Next. The Install Programs Wizard searches for an installation program, usually SETUP.EXE or INSTALL.EXE, and displays the command line in the Run Installation Program dialog box.

   If the Wizard did not find a program, you must choose Browse to locate it, and then choose Open to insert the selected file name in the Wizard.

5. Choose Finish to continue with the installation.

NOTE Names of installed Windows 95 programs appear in the list box in the Add/Remove Programs Properties sheet's Install/Uninstall page. If you want to uninstall a program, you can select it from the list. (See also "Removing: Windows Applications.")

Although you can use the Install Programs Wizard to install Windows 3.1 programs, they will not appear in this list for removal. You must use the program's own uninstall utility, if it exists, or a third party uninstall program. ▪

MS-DOS Prompt: Controlling the Session

Windows 95 offers enhanced MS-DOS support for running DOS applications, utilities, and games. You can run these programs by starting an MS-DOS prompt session within Windows.

> **CAUTION**   Don't run anything in a Windows MS-DOS session that alters system-critical files, such as the File Allocation Table. For example, don't run disk defragmenters, undelete, or unerase utilities. Use Windows 95 versions of these utilities instead.

Steps

1. Choose Start, Programs, MS-DOS Prompt.

2. At the command prompt, type DOS commands or start a DOS application.

3. Use the toolbar buttons to perform any of the following functions within the MS-DOS Prompt window: choose a font, mark text, copy text, paste text, switch to full screen, change MS-DOS prompt properties, switch window to background, change font properties.

4. Close DOS applications and then close the MS-DOS session by clicking the Close button in the upper-right corner of the MS-DOS Prompt window.

5. If any DOS applications are still open, Windows warns you and allows you to terminate the program by choosing Yes, or return to the session by choosing No.

NOTE   It is recommended that you close the DOS applications and not "crash" out by terminating the MS-DOS Prompt session. ▪

TIP   Press Alt+Enter to toggle a DOS session between windowed and full screen modes.

(See also "Starting Programs: MS-DOS Applications.")

APPLICATIONS AND ACCESSORIES

Navigating: Menus and Commands

Finding your way around menus and commands in Windows applications is easy, and should be done the same way in every properly designed Windows program. You can navigate menus and commands using the mouse or keyboard.

Steps

1. Open an application and click a menu, such as Edit. The commands for that menu drop down.

2. Move the mouse pointer left or right along the menu bar to drop down other menus if you want to browse the commands.

3. To choose a command on a menu, click it.

You will notice the following features on the menus.

- If the command appears gray on the menu, it is disabled—not available for the current situation. For example, the Edit menu's Copy command is grayed unless you have selected something to copy.

- If the command has a black, right arrowhead to the right of it, a submenu drops down automatically when you point to that command.

- If the command name is followed by an ellipsis (...), selecting the command displays a dialog box with a selection of options.

- If the command name is followed by a shortcut, you can alternatively use the keyboard shortcut for the command. For example, Ctrl+V is the shortcut shown for the Paste command on the Edit menu.

- All commands have an underlined letter. You can press that letter on the keyboard to choose the command.

 TIP Microsoft Office 97 applications display icons to the left of some commands, identical to the toolbar buttons that can be used for the commands.

Navigating: Scrolling a Document

Most Windows applications include a vertical scroll bar on the right side of the screen and a horizontal scroll bar on the bottom of the screen. You use the scroll bars to view a part of the document window that is not currently visible.

Steps

1. Open an application that has vertical and horizontal scroll bars, such as Microsoft Word or WordPad.

2. To scroll a short distance, click the arrow at either end of the scroll bar to move in the direction the arrow points. Use the vertical scroll bar to scroll up and down. Use the horizontal scroll bar to scroll left and right.

3. To scroll a longer distance, click in the gray area next to the arrow or drag the scroll bar box to a new location.

 TIP When you scroll a document using the scroll bars, the insertion point remains at the same place in the document and can scroll out of view. If you want to move the insertion point, click a new position.

Notepad: Using

Notepad is used for viewing or editing unformatted ASCII text files. Because Notepad stores files in text format, almost all word processing programs can open Notepad's files.

> **CAUTION** Notepad presents a warning message if you try to open a file that is too large for Notepad to hold. In that case, you can open the file in WordPad.

Steps

1. Choose Start, Programs, Accessories, Notepad. The Notepad window is displayed.

2. Type and edit text as desired. You must press Enter at the end of each line, or choose Edit, Word Wrap to cause text to wrap.

3. Choose File, Save to name and save the file.

(See also "WordPad: Editing a Document" and "Closing a Document: Saving.")

TIP   Type **.LOG** at the top of a Notepad document to have Notepad enter the current time and date at the end of the document each time you open the file. Alternatively, you can press F5 or choose Edit, Time/Date to insert the date and time at the insertion point.

Opening a Document: From Explorer

Windows Explorer is similar to the File Manager in Windows 3.1, but is much more powerful. You can use Explorer to find any document on your computer and then open a document, allowing the associated application to start simultaneously. If the associated application is already running, the document opens in that application.

Steps

1. Choose Start, Programs, Windows Explorer.

2. In the left pane, select the folder that contains the program or document that you want to open. Click the + next to the folder name to display subfolders of a folder. You must click the folder icon to display the files that belong to a folder.

3. In the right pane, double-click the icon next to the document that you want to open. The document opens in the associated application.

TROUBLESHOOTING   **I double-clicked a file in Explorer, but the Open With dialog box displayed, asking which program should be used to open the file.** The file you chose did not have an association in Windows. Choose from the list which program you want to use to open the file. If you do not know which program to use, you can try instead to open the file in a similar type of application. For example, if you know the file is a word processing file, open a word processing application and then try to open the file within the application. The converters in the application may be able to convert the file.

(See also "Files and Folders: Viewing in Explorer" in the "Disk and File Management" part of the book.)

Opening a Document: From My Computer

The My Computer icon on the Windows desktop is an alternative to using Explorer to view and open files. The display in My Computer differs in that it does not show the tree of drives and folders in a separate window pane. There is a single window in which you see only the subfolders or files in the currently selected folder. You might find My Computer handy for opening a document, but Explorer is better for many other file operations between folders, such as drag and drop.

Steps

1. Double-click the My Computer icon on the desktop.
2. Double-click the drive icon where the document is stored.
3. Double-click the folder that contains the document, and continue clicking subfolders as needed to locate the document.
4. Double-click the document to open it in the associated application.

Opening a Document: From Start Menu

Windows stores the name of the most recently opened documents for display on the Start menu's Documents menu. If your document is on the menu, you can open it quickly using this method.

Steps

1. Choose Start, Documents.
2. Click the document's name or icon on the menu. The document opens in the associated application.

TIP   To clear the list of documents on the Documents menu, choose Start, Settings, Taskbar. On the Start Menu Programs page of the Taskbar Properties sheet, click the Clear button and then click OK.

Paint: Creating Custom Colors

The color palette in Paint has 48 colors and allows you to add up to 16 custom colors. Custom colors you create in Paint apply only to Paint and are not automatically available in other applications. You can, however, use the color number settings to create the same color in applications that allow you to create custom colors.

Steps

1. Choose Start, Programs, Accessories, Paint to open Paint.

2. Choose Options, Edit Colors. In the Edit Colors dialog box click Define Custom Colors.

3. In the large color matrix box on the right side of the dialog box, click and drag with the mouse until the approximate color you want appears in the Color/Solid box.

4. In the luminosity bar at the far right, drag the arrow up or down to adjust the brightness of the color.

5. Click the Add to Custom Colors button to add this color to the Custom Colors palette. Choose the custom color and then click OK to close the Edit Colors dialog box.

TIP   If you want a solid color—rather than blended—double-click the right side of the Color/Solid box when the correct color is displayed.

TIP   If you know a color's numbers, you can specify the numbers in the Hue, Sat, Lum, Red, Green, and Blue boxes. These settings are found in the Edit Colors dialog box, under the Define Custom Colors option.

Paint: Creating Special Effects

With Windows Paint you can flip, rotate, stretch, skew, invert, and resize Paint objects. All of these effects are accessible on the Image menu.

Steps

1. Choose Start, Programs, Accessories, Paint to open Paint. Create an object or open the Paint file to which you want to add special effects.

2. Select an object using the Select tool in the Paint tool box.

3. From the Image menu, choose any of the following commands to add a special effect.

Creating Special Paint Effects

Choose This Command	To Create This Effect
Flip/Rotate	Flip a selection horizontally or vertically. Rotate the selection by 90, 180, or 270 degrees.
Stretch/Skew	Stretch or skew a selection horizontally or vertically the number of degrees you enter.
Invert Colors	Change to the opposite colors on the red/green/blue color wheel.
Attributes	Resize the image area, choosing Width, Height, Units of Measurement (Inches, Cm, Pels), and Colors or Black and White.

TIP You can also flip, stretch, or invert colors by right-clicking a selected object and choosing commands from the shortcut menu.

Paint: Embedding a Paint Object

Because Paint is an OLE *server* application, you can create objects that can be embedded in a document created by

APPLICATIONS AND ACCESSORIES

another Windows application, such as Word or WordPad. After a painting is embedded in a document, you can edit the painting from within the document. For this example, we will use a WordPad document.

Steps

1. Choose Start, Programs, Accessories, WordPad to open a WordPad document. Type some text in the document and then press Enter at least once to move the insertion point to a new line after the text.

2. Choose Insert, Object and select the Create New option button in the Insert Object dialog box.

3. In the Object Type list, select Bitmap Image and then choose OK. The Paint menus and tools appear within WordPad.

4. Draw a painting within the embedded box and then return to the WordPad document by clicking in the document, outside the painting.

5. Save the WordPad document. The embedded Paint object is saved with the document.

(See also "Closing a Document: Saving.")

NOTE The embedded Paint object can be edited at any time within the WordPad document by double-clicking the painting. You can embed an existing Paint object in a document by choosing Create From File in the Insert Object dialog box. ▓

(See also "Sharing: Using Object Linking and Embedding (OLE).")

Paint: Linking a Paint Object

Linking an object goes a step beyond embedding by automatically updating the linked object within documents that contain the object. If you link a painting to several documents, changes in the original painting will automatically update all of the documents that depend on that painting.

Steps

1. Choose Start, Programs, Accessories, Paint. Create and save a painting you want to link to other documents. You must save the painting for the link to work.

2. Open a word processing application, such as WordPad, and create a document.

3. In WordPad, choose Insert, Object. Select the Create From File option button and then click Browse.

4. Select the file containing the painting you want to link. Choose Insert.

5. Click the Link check box and then choose OK. The painting appears in the document. Save and close the document.

It is important that you click the Link check box in order for the Paint object to be linked to—not only embedded in—the document. As with embedded objects, linked objects can be edited within the *client* document by double-clicking the object. Changes to the object will cause any document linked to the same object file to be updated when the document is opened.

TROUBLESHOOTING   I followed the steps to create the link, but the painting in the document was not updated automatically. In the WordPad document, choose Edit, Links. In the Links dialog box, choose Update Now. To automatically update the link, be sure the Automatic option button is selected in the Links dialog box. Choose Close to close the Links dialog box.

In Windows 95, version 4.00.950 B, you may find it necessary to update the link in this way even though it should have been updated automatically. (To check your version of Windows, right-click the My Computer icon, choose Properties, and look at the System entry on the General page.)

(See also "Sharing: Using Object Linking and Embedding (OLE).")

APPLICATIONS AND ACCESSORIES

Paint: Using the Paint Toolbox

Use the Windows 95 Paint accessory to create, edit, and save bitmapped image files. The Paint toolbox contains the tools you need to create and modify a picture.

Steps

1. Choose Start, Programs, Accessories, Paint to open Paint.

2. At the left side of the Paint window, click to select the tool you want to use. Tips appear when you point to a tool, both next to the tool and in the status bar.

3. Position the tool's pointer where you want to begin the drawing.

4. Press and hold down the mouse button as you drag the mouse, and then release the mouse to stop drawing.

Exceptions to these steps for using Paint tools are:

- Paint Fill tool—Point and click.

- Text tool—Click and type.

- Curve tool—Click, drag, and click.

 TIP Choose Help, Help Topics for more details about the usage of each of the tools.

Removing: All Documents from the Documents Menu

A menu of shortcuts to the 15 most recently opened documents is displayed on the Start, Documents menu. If you want to clear the list—maybe you no longer access some of the documents or have moved or deleted them—you can clear the entire list.

Steps

1. Choose Start, Settings, Taskbar.

2. Click the Start Menu Programs page of the Taskbar Properties sheet.

3. Click the Clear button. The Documents menu is cleared. Click OK.

TIP Remove individual document shortcuts from the Documents menu by deleting them from the \Windows\Recent folder. The shortcut is moved to the Recycle Bin.

Removing: MS-DOS Applications

You can remove MS-DOS applications from your computer by using MS-DOS prompt commands, however a simpler way is to use Windows Explorer. Explorer is also the safer way to remove applications because the deleted files are stored in the Recycle Bin where they can be retrieved—until you empty the Recycle Bin. Applications and files removed at the MS-DOS prompt do not appear in the Recycle Bin.

WARNING Before deleting the folder containing the DOS application, check for files and subfolders that contain your personal data. If you want to keep these files, move them before removing the application or they may be lost. Also, be sure the folder was created just for this application and does not contain other critical files.

Steps

1. Choose Start, Programs, Windows Explorer to open Explorer.

2. Click the application's folder in the left pane.

3. Click the Delete button in the toolbar.

4. Windows asks you to confirm that you want to remove the folder and move all its contents to the Recycle Bin. Choose Yes to remove the folder.

TIP You can also drag the application's folder to the Recycle Bin on the desktop (or within Explorer) to remove the MS-DOS application.

APPLICATIONS AND ACCESSORIES

NOTE If the MS-DOS application you removed has a shortcut on the Start menu or desktop, you should remove it. (See "Removing: Start Menu Shortcuts and Folders.") ▓

If you want to restore any files you have moved to the Recycle Bin, see "Files: Restoring Deleted" in the "Disk and File Management" part of this book.

Removing: Start Menu Shortcuts and Folders

After you remove an application from your computer, you should remove any shortcuts that pointed to the application. If the shortcut is on the desktop, you can remove it by dragging it to the Recycle Bin on the desktop. To remove a shortcut from the Start menu, you use the Taskbar Properties sheet.

Steps
1. Choose Start, Settings, Taskbar.
2. Click the Start Menu Programs page of the Taskbar Properties sheet.
3. Choose Remove to open the Remove Shortcuts/Folders dialog box.
4. Select the folder or shortcut you want to delete. Expand the display as needed to locate the shortcut by clicking the + next to the folder.
5. Choose Remove and then click Close. Click Cancel or OK to close the Taskbar Properties sheet.

Removing: Windows Applications

Removing a Windows application can be complicated because most Windows programs have support files that are installed in the Windows subfolders, not together in the application's folder. Many Windows programs include a utility to uninstall the program or use Setup programs with an uninstall option. Use these uninstall utilities to remove Windows 3.1 applications.

Windows 95 has improved the process of removing a Windows 95 application by using the Add/Remove Programs Wizard to identify every component of the application you are removing. Only applications that provide uninstall programs designed to run in Windows 95 appear in the list for removal.

> **CAUTION**   The uninstall program should *not* remove your personal files, even if they are stored in the application's folders. The files deleted during the automatic uninstall are not moved to the Recycle Bin. To avoid losing your files, you should move files you want to keep before removing the application.

Steps

1. Choose Start, Settings, Control Panel to open the Control Panel.

2. Double-click the Add/Remove Programs icon.

3. Select the program's name in the Install/Uninstall page of the Add/Remove Programs Properties sheet.

4. Choose Add/Remove. If prompted, confirm that you want to continue to uninstall the application.

5. Answer any other prompts the uninstall utility presents for removing the program or a portion of the program. Some programs, such as Microsoft Word, may require you to insert the installation disks or CD to perform the uninstall. After the uninstall, choose Cancel to close the Add/Remove Programs Properties sheet, and then close the Control Panel.

When you remove Windows 95 applications following these steps, the applications should no longer appear on the Start menu or as a desktop shortcut icon. If they were not removed, see "Removing: Start Menu Shortcuts and Folders."

Selecting: Objects

Before you can perform a command to affect an *object* in a document, you must select the object to which the command applies. After the object is selected, you can copy, move, resize, format, or change the object in whatever way the application allows.

Steps

1. Display the object you want to select.

2. Click the object. Selection handles—little black boxes—should appear around the border of the object to indicate that it is selected.

NOTE Depending on the application and type of object, you must click either the border of the object or the inside of the object to select it. To deselect a selected object, click outside of it, in another place in the document. ▣

Some applications allow you to select more than one object. This is usually accomplished by holding down the Ctrl key while clicking each object. Then, commands that you choose can affect all of the selected objects at once.

Selecting: Options from Dialog Boxes

Actions or choices that are not simple enough to accomplish with a single command are often displayed in groups in a dialog box. Dialog boxes contain various types of *controls*, the method by which the user selects options. Dialog boxes appear when you select a menu command that is followed by an ellipsis (...).

Steps

1. Open a Windows application, such as Microsoft Excel for Windows 95. (This example was selected to show many kinds of controls in a single dialog box.)

2. Choose Tools, Options, or another command that will display a dialog box. The Options dialog box is displayed. See Figure 2.

3. Change settings using the various controls in the dialog box, as described in the table following these steps.

4. Choose a command button such as OK or Cancel to complete or cancel the selections. Exit the application.

The following table tells how to select options using the dialog box controls illustrated in Figure 2.

Types of Dialog Box Controls

For This Control	Do This
Option buttons	Click one option button. The selected option button has a black dot in the center. To remove the selection, select a different option button in the same group.
Check box	Click a check box to turn it on. A check appears in the box when selected. You can choose any number of check boxes.
Text box	Click inside the text box. Type an entry in the box. Correct mistakes by pressing the Backspace or Delete key.
Dialog tab	Click a dialog tab to see another page of options.
Command button	Click a command button to complete the command, cancel the command, or open an additional dialog box for more options.
Spin box	Click the up arrow to increase the number or the down arrow to decrease the number.
List box	Click an item in the list box. If the list box has a scroll bar, scroll through the list and then click the item you want. A drop-down list box looks like a text box with a down arrow button next to it. Click the down arrow and then click an item in the list.

APPLICATIONS AND ACCESSORIES

Check boxes

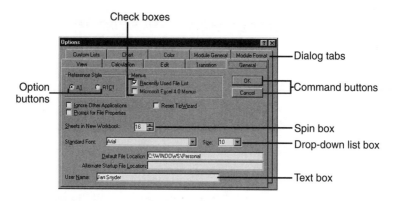

Dialog tabs

Option buttons

Command buttons

Spin box

Drop-down list box

Text box

FIGURE 2
Select controls in the Options dialog box to choose options.

Selecting: Text in Documents

Before you can work with existing text to format it or copy it, you must first select it using the mouse or keyboard. Selected text usually appears in reverse colors. For example, for black text on a white background, selected text is white on a black background.

Steps

1. Position the I-beam at the beginning of the text that you want to select.

2. Hold down the left mouse button, drag to the end of the text you want to select, and then release the mouse button. The entire selection should appear in reverse colors.

TIP   You can select text using the keyboard by holding down the Shift key and pressing the arrow keys.

After text is selected, you can apply formatting. For example, click the Bold button to bold the selected text.

TIP   To select a word, double-click the word. To select text that extends beyond the screen, drag to the lower edge of the screen where selection continues during scrolling.

Sharing: Transferring Data Using File Converters

Many Windows applications include built-in file converters that are designed to open files created in other programs. For example, you may want to convert a WordPerfect file to Word. Ideally, file converters preserve as much as possible of the document's text formatting and special elements. Whatever is not converted cleanly, you may need to edit after the conversion.

Steps

1. Start the application to which you want to convert the file. (To convert to Word, start Word.)

2. Click the Open button to display the Open dialog box. Or, if you are importing another file type into an existing file, choose Insert, File to display the Insert File dialog box.

3. In the Files of Type drop-down list, choose the type of file you are converting from. (To convert from WordPerfect, select the version of WordPerfect from the list.) If you are uncertain what type of file you are converting, select All Files (*.*).

4. Locate and open the file. The status bar shows the progress of the conversion, which may take only a second for a small file, or longer for a large file.

Instead of opening the file you want to convert into a different application, you can convert the file in its original application by saving it as the other file type. For example, in WordPerfect, you can choose File, Save As and then choose a version of Word in the Save As Type drop-down list.

NOTE File converters are sometimes a custom option in a program's setup. If you have trouble converting a file, you may have to run setup again to install the specific file converter needed for the conversion. ▪

Sharing: Using Object Linking and Embedding (OLE)

OLE technology was designed by Microsoft to allow creation of *compound documents*. You create a document in one application, but link or embed objects from other applications into the document.

To *embed* an object, simply copy from one document and paste it into another (both documents must support OLE). The embedded object can be edited within the application where it is placed, without leaving the application. (See "Clipboard: Copying Data.") To *link* the object so that the client document is updated when the object changes, use the following steps.

Steps

1. Open the *server* document—the one that contains the information you want to link—and select the object to be linked.

2. Choose <u>E</u>dit, <u>C</u>opy, or click the Copy button.

3. Open the *client* document—the one where you want the information to appear—and then click where you want to place the information.

4. Choose <u>E</u>dit, Paste <u>S</u>pecial.

5. In the <u>A</u>s list box, select a format. Click Paste <u>L</u>ink and choose OK.

NOTE   Paste <u>L</u>ink may be disabled in some applications that do not support this feature. For example, you may not be able to use Paste <u>L</u>ink to link a bitmap image. The option is dimmed, therefore you cannot select the check box. ▩

The linked object is embedded, therefore allowing you to access the server application within the client document. It also is linked, meaning that whenever the object is changed—by whatever method—the document to which it is linked will automatically be updated with the new version of the object. If the automatic update option is turned off, you are prompted when you open the document to update the links.

TIP To edit an embedded or linked object, double-click it. The server application opens within the client application. For some objects, such as sound objects, double-clicking runs the object instead of allowing editing. For this kind of object, right-click and select a command for editing the object.

(See also "Paint: Embedding a Paint Object" and "Paint: Linking a Paint Object.")

Shortcuts: Changing Shortcut Properties

Desktop icons, called *shortcuts*, are just that—shortcuts for starting applications. Shortcuts are an alternative to locating programs on menus and submenus. You can change the following shortcut properties.

- *Target*.   Change the file that the shortcut opens.
- *Start In*.   Start the program in a different folder.
- *Shortcut Key*.   Add shortcut keys that activate the shortcut.
- *Run*.   Run the program in a normal, maximized, or minimized window.
- *Change Icon*.   Change the icon used for the shortcut.

Steps

1. Right-click the shortcut icon and then choose Properties to display the General page of the Shortcut Properties sheet.

2. Click the Shortcut tab.

3. Choose the property you want to change (see the previous list).

4. Choose Apply to keep the changes. Choose OK to save the changes and close the Shortcut Properties sheet.

Shortcuts: Creating on Desktop

Although most of the applications you use are listed on the Start and Programs menus, you may find it easier to start your application, or open a document by using a shortcut icon on the desktop. If your application did not create a shortcut icon when you installed the application, you can create the shortcut icon yourself.

If you have a favorite document that you open frequently, you can place a shortcut icon for the document on the desktop. Double-clicking the shortcut icon starts the application. For document shortcut icons, the associated application is started and that document is opened in the application.

Steps

1. Choose Start, Programs, Windows Explorer to open Explorer.

2. Locate the application or document for which you want to create a shortcut.

3. Right-drag the file onto the desktop, then release the right mouse button. (Right-dragging is dragging while holding down the right mouse button.) A shortcut menu appears.

4. Choose Create Shortcut(s) Here from the shortcut menu. The shortcut icon is placed on the desktop.

TIP   You also can move existing shortcuts from the Start menu to the desktop. Right-click the taskbar and choose Properties. Click the Start Menu Programs tab and then click Advanced. Locate the folder in the left pane of the Exploring window. In the right pane, shortcuts appear. To copy the application's shortcut to the desktop, hold down the Ctrl key and then drag and drop the shortcut onto the desktop. (Holding down the Ctrl key copies instead of moving, so the original shortcut will remain on the Start menu.)

(See also "Copying and Moving: Drag and Drop.")

Starting Programs: At Startup

If there are certain applications you want to run every time you turn on your computer, you can add them to the Startup folder.

Programs in the Startup folder appear in the Startup menu, a submenu of the Programs menu.

Steps

1. Choose Start, Settings, Taskbar.

2. Select the Start Menu Programs tab and click Add.

3. Click Browse and then double-click folders until you find the folder in which the program is located. Double-click the program file and then click Next.

4. Double-click the Startup folder (you will probably need to scroll down to it).

5. Accept the title in the Select a Name for the Shortcut text box or type a new title. Click Finish.

 TIP If you create a Startup folder shortcut icon on your desktop, you can use the right mouse button to drag and drop program or document files from Explorer into the Startup folder.

To remove a program from the Startup folder, see "Program Menu: Removing Items" in the "Customizing Windows 95" part of this book.

Starting Programs: From Explorer

With Explorer, you can locate any file on your computer. You can also start programs using Explorer instead of using menus or shortcut icons.

 TIP Start Explorer by right-clicking the Start menu and choosing Explore.

Steps

1. Choose Start, Programs, Windows Explorer to open Explorer.

 2. In the left pane, select the folder that contains the program you want to start. Click the + next to the folder name to display subfolders of a folder. You must click the folder icon to display the files that belong to a folder.

APPLICATIONS AND ACCESSORIES

3. In the right pane, double-click the icon next to the application file that you want to open. The application starts.

Starting Programs: From Shortcut Icon

Most applications you install place an entry on the Start menu or Programs submenu. You can create a shortcut icon on your desktop that allows you to start programs.

TIP Shortcut icons can be created for opening documents too. (See "Shortcuts: Creating on Desktop.")

Steps

1. Open the Windows Explorer by choosing Start, Programs, Windows Explorer.

2. Locate and select the program file for which you want to create a shortcut.

3. Right-click the file name and choose Copy.

4. Right-click the desktop and choose Paste Shortcut.

(See also "Files and Folders: Viewing in Explorer" in the "Disk and File Management" part of this book.)

Starting Programs: From Start Menu

The Start menu's Programs menu is probably the simplest way to start applications. Desktop shortcut icons may not be in view because of running applications, and it's sometimes hard to locate the correct starting file in Explorer. The Programs menu is always accessible and organized. Groups and folders are listed alphabetically, followed by additional non-grouped applications listed alphabetically.

NOTE Generally, when you install an application, its group, folder, or application name is added to the Programs menu for you. Some programs, such as Corel WordPerfect Suite 7, install directly on the Start menu instead of one level down on the Programs menu. ■

Steps

1. Choose Start, Programs. The Programs menu appears next to the Start menu.

2. Point to the application's group, folder, or name on the menu. Applications in groups or folders are listed with an arrow—when you point to them, a submenu opens. If the item you want is on a submenu, point to it. The item you point to is highlighted.

3. Click to start the application.

You can add, change, or remove items from the Start menu or Programs menu. (See "Start Menu: Changing Items" and similar tasks in the "Customizing Windows 95" part of this book.)

Starting Programs: MS-DOS Applications

If you know that your installed DOS application can run in a window, then start it from the Start menu or double-click the application name in Windows Explorer. You also can run the application in MS-DOS mode or at the MS-DOS prompt.

Steps

1. Choose Start, Programs, MS-DOS Prompt to start an MS-DOS prompt session.

2. At the DOS prompt, type the CD command to move to the folder of the program you want to start. For example, type **CD \"Program Files"**. (Note that you must enclose long folder names in quotes in DOS, or use the short name, such as **CD \progra~1**.)

3. Press Enter. At the DOS prompt, type the command to start the application and then press Enter.

(See also "Installing: MS-DOS Applications," "MS-DOS Prompt: Controlling the Session," and "Switching: To MS-DOS Mode.")

NOTE To successfully run a DOS application, you may need to change the application's properties. Right-click the application's shortcut icon and then choose Properties to open the Properties sheet. Review the settings, using the Help button as needed for more detail about the settings. ▪

APPLICATIONS AND ACCESSORIES

Switching: Between Applications

Windows 95 makes it easy to switch between applications that are running. Each application is represented by a button on the taskbar, plainly labeled with the program's icon, name, and perhaps a document name. Even if you minimize an application's window, the taskbar button remains.

Steps

1. Open the applications you want to use. Each one displays a button on the taskbar.

2. Click a button for any application you want to switch to.

TIP   Press Alt+Tab to switch between two applications. If more than two applications are running, switch by holding down Alt, and then pressing Tab repeatedly until you see the application you want selected in the selection window that appears. Release the Alt key to switch to that application.

If your application windows are not all maximized, you can switch applications by clicking a part of the open window.

Switching: Between Document Windows

In many applications, you can open more than one document and switch between them. You can choose File, Open more than once, opening each document in its own document window. If the documents are not maximized to full screen, simply click the window of the document you want to switch to.

Steps

1. Choose the Window menu.

2. Choose the document's file name from the Window menu or type the number that precedes the file name on the Window menu.

TIP   You can also switch document windows by repeatedly pressing Ctrl+F6.

Switching: From MS-DOS Mode

If you are running in MS-DOS mode, you need to know how to get back to the properties sheet to discontinue the MS-DOS mode setting. (See also "Switching: To MS-DOS Mode.")

Steps

1. Restart Windows following the MS-DOS mode session, then open Explorer and locate the \Windows\Start Menu\Programs folder.

2. Right-click the icon for the MS-DOS Prompt program and choose Properties.

3. Select the Program tab, then click the Advanced button.

4. Uncheck the MS-DOS Mode check box and choose OK twice.

Switching: To MS-DOS Mode

To run MS-DOS applications that don't seem to run correctly in Windows, you may be able to configure the program's properties, or you may need to switch to MS-DOS mode, which shuts down all applications and Windows while running the DOS application.

When to Use MS-DOS Mode

Before you try to run the program in MS-DOS mode, try these other options within Windows.

- Check the program's documentation for special memory requirements or other settings. Change the program's property settings accordingly and try to run the program.

- Open the application in a window (if possible) and then press Alt+Enter to run the application in full-screen mode.

If you still cannot make the program run correctly, then try MS-DOS mode.

APPLICATIONS AND ACCESSORIES

Steps

1. Create a shortcut icon for the DOS application.
2. Right-click the shortcut icon and then choose Properties.
3. Select the Program tab and then choose Advanced.
4. Select the Prevent MS-DOS-Based Programs from Detecting Windows check box. Choose OK.

TROUBLESHOOTING **I tried the Prevent MS-DOS-Based Programs from Detecting Windows option and my DOS application still won't run.** In the previous Step 4, select the MS-DOS Mode check box and try running the application again.

WordPad: Creating or Opening a Document

WordPad is the accessory word processor that comes with Windows. It has more features than Notepad—such as formatting—and allows you to open larger documents than Notepad does.

Steps

1. Choose Start, Programs, Accessories, WordPad to open WordPad.

   WordPad opens with a new document. You can begin typing in the new document or open an existing document.

2. Click the Open button on the toolbar. If the file is on a different disk, select the drive in the Look In drop-down list.
3. Double-click the folder that contains the file. Continue to double-click subfolders as needed to locate the file.
4. In the Files of Type drop-down list, select the type of files you want to list.
5. Double-click the file you want to open, or type its name in the File Name text box and click Open.

You can work on only one document at a time in WordPad. If you open another document, the displayed document closes.

If you haven't saved changes, WordPad prompts you to save the changes.

TIP To work on more than one WordPad document, start the WordPad application multiple times.

NOTE WordPad saves files in Microsoft Word for Windows 6.0 format. You may want to save the file in a different format, such as plain text for a batch file, or to import into an HTML document for a Web page. If you want to save the file as a text file, choose Text Document in the Save as Type drop-down list in the Save As dialog box. (See also "Closing a Document: Saving.") ■

WordPad: Editing a Document

In WordPad, you edit text the same way you edit text in other documents—by placing the insertion point and typing or deleting text.

Steps

1. Position the insertion point where you want to change text.
2. To insert text, type. To delete text, press Backspace to delete characters to the left of the insertion point, or press Delete to delete characters to the right.

TIP If you change your mind about an edit you just made, click the Undo button to undo the most recent change. If you don't like the result, click Undo again to return the text to the way it was before the previous Undo.

If your edits require changing a word, sentence, or paragraph, then you can simplify editing by first selecting the text you want to move or change. (See also "Selecting: Text in Documents.")

APPLICATIONS AND ACCESSORIES

WordPad: Formatting

WordPad offers the following types of formatting features that allow you to add interest to your document.

- Character formatting—font, point size, bold, italic, and underline.
- Paragraph formatting—alignment of paragraphs and headings.
- Document formatting—margins, page size, and orientation.

For character or paragraph formatting, you'll generally use the following steps. Document formatting is accomplished using menu commands, as described in the following table.

Steps

1. Select the text to be formatted.
2. Choose a command from the Format menu or a button on the Format toolbar.

The following table shows some of the formatting options available for characters, paragraphs, and documents in WordPad.

Formatting a WordPad Document

Choose This	To Apply This Format
Font drop-down list	Change font
Font size drop-down list	Change font size
B	Bold
I	Italic
U	Underline
🖉	Color text

Choose This	To Apply This Format
	Align paragraph at left
	Center paragraph
	Align paragraph at right
	Bullet precedes each paragraph
Format, Tabs	Set tabs for the document
File, Page Setup	Set paper size and source, orientation, and margins for the document

APPLICATIONS AND ACCESSORIES

Customizing Windows 95

Windows 95 gives you almost endless ability to customize features for optimal productivity and performance. You can control how your display looks; change date and time formats, languages, keyboard and mouse settings; and customize the taskbar.

Many of the items you can customize are accessed on the Control Panel. This part of the book describes several of these items, but others, such as multimedia and network settings, are found in their own parts of this book.

Accessibility: Settings for the Impaired

Accessibility properties are included in Windows 95 to make computers more available to the millions of people with hearing, sight, and movement disabilities. You can adjust the sound, display, keyboard, and mouse interface. Each property is described in the Accessibility Properties sheet.

Steps

1. Choose Start, Settings, Control Panel to open the Control Panel.

2. Double-click the Accessibility Options icon to open the Accessibility Properties sheet.

3. Select each tab, choose options, and then click OK.

TROUBLESHOOTING   I don't see the Accessibility Options icon in the Control Panel. You need to install it in Windows Setup. (See also "Windows Components: Adding and Removing.")

Customizing: Settings for Each User

If you share a computer with someone else, you can set up user profiles to store each person's custom settings. Each user has a logon name that activates custom settings when Windows is reset.

Steps

1. Choose Start, Settings, Control Panel, and then double-click the Passwords icon.

2. Click the User Profiles tab. If all users (or just you) use the same preferences, the first option is already selected: All Users of This PC.

3. Select the Users Can Customize Their Preferences option button.

   The User Profile Settings section becomes available when you click this option.

4. If you want to include the following items in each user's profile, check the corresponding check box.

   *Include Desktop Icons and Network Neighborhood Contents in User Settings

   *Include Start Menu and Program Groups in User Settings

5. Choose OK. You will be prompted to restart your computer for the changes to take effect. Choose Yes to restart your computer.

NOTE After you follow the previous steps, each user who logs on can customize his or her own settings. If other users share the computer, each user should log off when he or she is finished using the computer. Log off by choosing Start, Shut Down, and then select Close All Programs and Log On as a Different User. Choose Yes. ▉

(See also "Security: Setting Up Passwords.")

Customizing: The Keyboard

You can change keyboard properties to set the character re-peat rate, cursor blink rate, the language, and the keyboard type. You can select multiple languages for your keyboard and switch between them.

Steps

1. Choose Start, Settings, Control Panel, and then double-click the Keyboard icon.

2. On the Keyboard Properties sheet, click one of the tabs described in the following table to make changes.

3. Click Apply to accept changes as you go, or click OK to accept the changes and close the Keyboard Properties sheet. You may be prompted to restart the computer for the changes to take effect.

Keyboard Properties	
Tab	**Description**
Speed	Drag the sliders to set Repeat Delay, Repeat Rate, and Cursor Blink Rate. You can use the text box to test the repeat rate before accepting the change.
Language	Select a language in the Language list box to change languages. Click Add to add another language to the list. Choose Properties to select a keyboard layout for the selected language. Click Remove to delete a language from the list.
General	To choose a different keyboard, click the Change button. Make changes in the Select Device dialog box that appears.

NOTE   Changing the keyboard language does not change the language used by Windows; for that, you must purchase a different language version of Windows. ■

CUSTOMIZING WINDOWS 95

TIP   Choose Enable Indicator on Taskbar on the Language page to place an indicator on the taskbar. Click the indicator to pop up a menu of languages from the Language list. Click a language to switch to that keyboard.

(See also "Keyboard: Configuring" in the "Equipment Configuration" part of this book.)

Customizing: The Mouse

You can change the behavior of your mouse and its pointers in the Mouse Properties sheet. If you are left-handed, you may want to change the button assignments.

Steps

1. Choose Start, Settings, Control Panel, and then double-click the Mouse icon.

2. On the Mouse Properties sheet, click a tab and make changes to the properties. Standard tabs are Buttons, Pointers, Motion, and General.

3. Click Apply to accept changes as you go, or click OK to accept the changes and close the Mouse Properties sheet.

NOTE   If you have another kind of pointing device, such as a touch pad, follow the manufacturer's instructions for installing it. The Mouse icon in the Control Panel may be replaced by the pointing device's custom icon. Double-click the icon to view the settings. ■

(See also "Mouse: Configuring Mouse Motion" and "Mouse: Changing Button Settings" in the "Equipment Configuration" part of this book.)

Customizing: The Send To Menu

The Send To menu can be used to move, fax, e-mail, print, and accomplish other actions with files and folders. To access the

Send To command, right-click a file or folder in Explorer or on the desktop.

Steps

1. In Explorer, open the \Windows\SendTo folder. Then open the folder that contains the item you want to send to the SendTo folder.

2. Using the right mouse button, drag and drop the item to the SendTo folder. The shortcut menu opens.

3. Click Create Shortcut(s) Here.

4. Open the SendTo folder to see the new entry. You can rename it if you desire.

TIP   Create a Send To item for a ZIP drive, additional printers, and commonly used folders.

Display: Changing Background Pattern or Wallpaper

To keep your desktop interesting, you can select a background pattern or wallpaper to display, and change the design whenever you like. You can use your own bitmap file, such as a logo, for wallpaper instead of the collection in Windows 95.

CAUTION   Generally, you choose a pattern or a wallpaper, but not both. If you have tiled the wallpaper over the entire screen, it covers the pattern selection. To see a pattern, select (None) in the Wallpaper list box.

Steps

1. Right-click the desktop and then choose Properties from the shortcut menu. The Display Properties sheet displays the Background page.

2. To choose a pattern, choose a design from the Pattern list box. A sample of the pattern appears on the sample display. Choose Apply if you want to see the pattern on the desktop.

CUSTOMIZING WINDOWS 95

If you want to edit the pattern to create your own pattern, click the Edit Pattern button.

3. To choose a wallpaper, choose a design from the Wallpaper list box. A sample of the wallpaper appears on the sample display. Choose Apply if you want to see the wallpaper on the desktop. Choose Tile to duplicate the wallpaper on the entire desktop; choose Center to display the wallpaper in the center of the desktop.

   To use your own .BMP type file as wallpaper, click Browse to select it.

4. Choose OK if you are finished with display settings.

NOTE   If you have the Microsoft Plus! product installed, you see a Plus! tab in the Display Properties sheet. Select the Stretch Desktop Wallpaper to Fit the Screen check box on the Plus! page to stretch a centered wallpaper to fill the screen. Try this with the Clouds wallpaper. ▨

TIP   Patterns take on the color set in the Appearance page of the Display Properties sheet. To give a pattern a new look, change the color. (See "Display: Changing Color Schemes.")

Display: Changing Color Schemes

Windows has a number of predefined color schemes, but you can also choose and save your own custom color schemes.

Steps

1. Right-click the desktop and choose Properties from the shortcut menu. On the Display Properties sheet, click the Appearance tab.

2. In the Scheme drop-down list, select a color and text scheme. The sample box changes to show how items in Windows will appear in the new scheme.

3. Choose OK to use the displayed color scheme, or continue with these steps to use the color scheme as a base for customizing parts of the scheme.

In the Item list, choose the screen element that you want to change. Or click an item in the sample box, which automatically selects the item's name in the Item list.

4. In the Size, Color, Font, Size, and Color lists, select new settings for the selected element. Notice also that you can click the Bold and Italic buttons for text items. Each time you make a change, the sample box displays it.

5. Choose Apply anytime you want to see the color scheme applied to Windows. To save the scheme so it will appear on the Scheme list, click Save As. Type a name, and then choose OK. Choose OK to change Windows to the currently displayed sample scheme.

TIP   To find additional colors, choose Other in the drop-down Color palette. Select a color from the expanded palette or create your own custom color. (See also "Paint: Creating Custom Colors" in the "Applications and Accessories" part of this book.)

Display: Changing Resolution, Font Size, and Color Palette

The screen resolution—the number of dots on the screen—is a display property you can change only if your monitor is capable of running in Super VGA 800 × 600 resolution or better. You also must select a Super VGA or better monitor type as described in these steps.

Steps

1. Right-click the desktop and then choose Properties from the shortcut menu. On the Display Properties sheet, click the Settings tab.

2. Click the Advanced Properties button and then select the Monitor tab.

    If you do not see an Advanced Properties button on the Settings page, refer to the Note following these steps.

    If your monitor type is not displayed, click the Change button. Select your monitor from the Models list or click

the Show All Devices option button to display a more
extensive list. If you are unsure, select (Standard
Monitor Types) in the Manufacturers list box and then
choose a Super VGA setting in the Models list. Choose
OK and Close to return to the Settings page.

3. Move the Desktop Area slider to the right toward More,
   until you see the desired pixel setting below (800 × 600
   pixels or greater).

4. If your monitor is capable of displaying 256 or more
   colors, choose the setting in the Color Palette drop-down
   list.

5. If you want to change the font size Windows uses,
   choose from Large Fonts or Small Fonts in the Font
   Size drop-down list. For more specific sizing, click the
   Custom button and choose, type, or drag a size on the
   ruler. Choose OK. Choose OK again to accept the
   changes. If you changed any setting besides Desktop
   Area, you will be prompted to restart your computer.

NOTE   These steps are based on Microsoft Windows 95,
version 4.00.950 A. If your version of Windows 95 is different,
your steps for this task will vary. To check your version of
Windows, right-click the My Computer icon, choose Properties,
and look at the System entry on the General page. ▪

NOTE   If your version of Windows displays a Change Display
Type button on the Settings page (see the previous Step 2), click
this button and continue with the instructions in Step 2 by
clicking the Change button, and so on. ▪

> **CAUTION**   Never try to select a monitor type that is beyond the
> capability of your monitor. You could cause damage to the monitor or
> make the display unreadable. If your selection made the screen
> unreadable, shut off the computer. Turn on the computer; press F8
> when you see the phrase "Starting Windows 95." Choose the Safe

Mode selection from the menu. When the Safe Mode Windows desktop is displayed, repeat the preceding steps, but choose a resolution you are certain your monitor can display.

TIP   Some programs, especially games, have peculiar display setting needs. If you frequently change these settings, select the Show Settings Icon on Taskbar check box on the Display Properties, Settings page. (This check box is not available in Windows 95 versions before 4.00.950b.) The Display icon appears next to the clock, allowing you to quickly make changes to the display by clicking the Display icon and selecting from the pop-up menu.

Display: Using Screen Savers

Screen savers display moving designs on the screen when you haven't typed or moved the mouse for a preset time.

Why Use a Screen Saver?

Screen savers were created to prevent the screen image from burning onto the screen if the display did not change frequently enough. This is rarely a problem with newer monitors, but screen savers can still be entertaining and hide the work on your screen when you leave your desk. You can even assign a password to the screen saver so that only you can reactivate the screen.

Steps

1. Right-click the desktop and then choose Properties from the shortcut menu. On the Display Properties sheet, click the Screen Saver tab.

2. Select a screen saver from the Screen Saver drop-down list. A sample of the screen saver appears on the sample display. For a full-screen view, click the Preview button. Click the screen to return from the preview. Try other screen savers from the list.

CUSTOMIZING WINDOWS 95

3. Change the properties of the selected screen saver by choosing Settings. Options available differ for each screen saver you choose, but usually include the speed and colors. Make selections and then choose OK.

4. In the Wait spin box, type or select the number of minutes you want the screen to be idle before the screen saver activates. Choose Apply to accept the settings, but keep the Display Properties sheet open.

5. If you want to set a password for reactivating the screen, click the Password Protected check box and then choose Change. In the Change Password dialog box, type the same password in each text box and then choose OK. Choose OK again for confirmation, and then choose OK to apply the changes and close the Display Properties sheet.

NOTE   If your monitor has energy-saving features, then you should see the Energy Star icon on the Screen Saver page of the Display Properties sheet. You can set the timing for the monitor to go into low-power standby by choosing the Low-power Standby check box and setting the number of minutes. Choose the Shut Off Monitor check box and set the number of minutes before the monitor is completely shut off. ■

TIP   If you want to use a screen saver that you have obtained from an outside source, install the screen saver to the \Windows\System folder so that it will appear as a choice in the Screen Saver drop-down list.

Fonts: Installing

Although Windows installs font files during setup, you may want to add additional fonts from the Windows disks or CD, from vendors, or even from online services.

Steps

1. Choose Start, Settings, Control Panel and then double-click the Fonts folder in Control Panel. The Fonts

window displays all of the fonts currently registered on the system.

2. To change the look of the font listing, choose View and then choose Large Icons, List, or Details. To simplify the list, you can also choose View, Hide Variations to hide the repetitive Bold and Italic variations.

3. Choose File, Install New Font to display the Add Fonts dialog box. Select the Drives and Folders lists to choose the location of the font you want to install.

4. Fonts available at the location you specified appear in the List of Fonts list box. Select the font(s) you want to add.

5. If you want to copy the fonts directly to the Windows Fonts folder, keep the Copy Fonts to Fonts Folder check box checked. Choose OK to add the fonts you selected.

TIP In Explorer, install fonts by dragging them from a disk and dropping them into the \Windows\Fonts folder. To be sure the fonts are entered correctly in the Registry, test by printing in the fonts you installed using drag and drop.

Fonts: Removing from the Hard Disk

You can delete font files installed in Windows, which also removes them from the Registry.

Steps

1. Choose Start, Settings, Control Panel and then double-click the Fonts folder in Control Panel. The Fonts window displays all of the fonts currently registered on the system.

2. Select the font(s) you want to delete.

3. Choose File, Delete. Windows asks if you're sure you want to delete these fonts. Choose Yes to delete. The font files are removed from the Registry and moved to the Recycle Bin.

CUSTOMIZING WINDOWS 95

TIP   Use Explorer to drag and drop fonts from the \Windows\Fonts folder to the Recycle Bin. If you make a mistake, recover the font from the Recycle Bin.

Help Topics: Adding Custom Notes

You can add notes to Help topics in Windows applications. You may want to include information specific to your preferred settings or formatting, or details about your company's templates for documents. Notes that you add are called *annotations*.

Steps

1. In Windows Help or a Windows application's Help system, display the topic that you want to annotate.
2. Click the Options button and then choose Annotate.
3. In the Annotate dialog box, type the notes that you want to attach to this Help topic.
4. Choose Save. A paper clip icon appears next to the topic title in the Help window.

To read an annotation, click the paper clip icon. To remove an annotation, click the paper clip icon and then choose Delete in the Annotate dialog box.

(See also "Help: On the Desktop" in the "Windows 95 Basics" part of this book.)

Installing: Unlisted Components

You can add and remove Windows components from your system, but at some time you may want to install a Windows component that is not listed in the Components list in the Windows Setup page of the Add/Remove Programs Properties sheet. The Windows 95 Resource Kit on the Windows 95 CD contains system management utilities you many want to add.

Steps

1. Choose Start, Settings, Control Panel and then double-click the Add/Remove Programs icon. Click the Windows Setup tab.

2. Click the Have Disk button at the bottom of the Windows Setup page.

3. In the Copy Manufacturer's Files From box, type the path to the setup information file (.INF file) for the Windows component that you want to install. Choose Browse if you need to look for the file, and then choose OK to select it.

4. In the Have Disk dialog box, check the items you want to install from the Components list. Choose Install.

5. Choose OK. The program you installed is added either to the Windows Setup Components list or to the list on the Install/Uninstall page of the Add/Remove Programs Properties sheet.

(See also "Windows Components: Adding and Removing.")

Properties: Setting for a Shortcut Icon

You can customize the action of a shortcut icon by changing its settings in the Properties sheet. You can set the target file, the folder to start in, the shortcut key, the window size, and the icon used for the shortcut.

Steps

1. On the desktop, right-click the shortcut icon and then choose Properties from the shortcut menu.

2. Click the Shortcut tab and then select the property you want to change. Choose OK to save the changes.

(See also "Shortcuts: Changing Shortcut Properties" and "Shortcuts: Creating on Desktop" in the "Applications and Accessories" part of this book.)

CUSTOMIZING WINDOWS 95

Properties Sheets: Using

You can customize almost anything in Windows, often with settings in its Properties sheets. Most of the icons in the Control Panel open Properties sheets. You can also find Properties sheets for files, folders, desktop icons, the taskbar, and the Recycle Bin.

Steps

1. Right-click the item for which you want to change or view properties.

2. Choose Properties in the shortcut menu. The Properties sheet is displayed.

3. View or make changes to properties, clicking tabs at the top to change pages. Choose OK to save changes to properties, or choose Cancel to close the Properties sheet without keeping changes.

Regional Settings: Customizing

By changing regional settings properties, you can switch between different international character sets, number formats, currency formats, and date and time displays. Changing the language and country formats does not change the language used in Windows features, but affects applications that take advantage of these features.

Steps

1. Choose Start, Settings, Control Panel. Double-click the Regional Settings icon to display the Regional Settings Properties sheet.

2. Click the tabs described in the following table and make the selections you want.

3. Click Apply to make the changes and keep the Regional Settings Properties sheet open to make additional changes. Choose OK to accept the changes and close the sheet.

Regional Settings

Tab	Description
Regional Settings	In the drop-down list, select the region you want to set. This selection changes settings in the other pages; therefore, you should set this property first.
Number	Notice the Appearance Samples boxes at the top that illustrate the number format according to the selections below. Make changes to the settings by choosing from their drop-down lists or by typing in the boxes. Observe the effects on the samples.
Currency	Change the currency properties by choosing from the drop-down lists or by typing in the boxes. Observe the effects on the Appearance samples.
Time	Change the style of the time by choosing from the drop-down lists or by typing in the boxes. The changes are shown in the Time Sample box.
Date	Change long date, short date, and date separator styles by choosing from the drop-down lists or by typing in the boxes. The changes are shown in the Long Date Sample box or the Short Date Sample box. These date formats will be the default formats in programs where you insert the date.

NOTE To type the currency symbols in an application, you may also have to change the language in the keyboard properties. (See "Customizing: The Keyboard.")

TIP Many Windows programs let you set currency and number formats that will override these regional settings. If you only need these formats temporarily or infrequently, you can change them in the application when they are needed.

CUSTOMIZING WINDOWS 95

Registry: Backing Up

Making changes to the Windows 95 *Registry*, where both Windows 95 configurations and application configurations are stored, is risky even for very experienced Windows users. Before you try to edit the Registry, you should back it up.

CAUTION   It is a good idea to back up the Registry before installing a Windows 95 application. Because programs write new information to the Registry during setup, the Registry is in jeopardy every time you install an application, even if the application displays the "Designed for Windows 95" logo.

TIP   The files you need to back up are SYSTEM.DAT and USER.DAT, both hidden files in the \Windows folder. If you want to use Explorer to copy the files, be sure Explorer is set to show hidden files. In Explorer, choose View, Options, select Show All Files, and click OK.

Steps

1. Microsoft recommends copying the Registry files while running Windows in Safe Mode. Restart your computer; when the Starting Windows 95 message appears, press F8. Choose Safe Mode Command Prompt Only from the menu.

2. Create a subfolder in the \Windows folder called Registry. Change to the \Windows folder. Type **attrib -h -s -r system.dat** and then press Enter. Type **attrib -h -s -r user.dat** and then press Enter.

   This unhides the Registry files so you can copy them.

3. Type **copy system.dat .\Registry** and then press Enter. Type **copy user.dat .\Registry** and then press Enter.

4. Type **attrib +h +s +r system.dat** and then press Enter. Type **attrib +h +s +r user.dat** and then press Enter.

   This hides the Registry files again.

5. Restart the computer.

TIP   If you back up the Registry frequently, you may want to put the attrib and copy commands from Steps 2 to 4 in a batch file—a text file you can run each time you want to copy the Registry files.

TIP   If you need to restore the Registry, start the computer in Safe Mode, copy the files from the \Windows\Registry folder back into the \Windows folder, then hide them again, as in the previous Step 4.

Registry: Using Registry Editor

All important configuration information is stored in the Windows 95 Registry. This includes the properties set in the Control Panel, settings installed by all of your Windows 95 applications, and hardware detected by the Add New Hardware Wizard and Plug and Play devices. You can also make changes directly in the Registry Editor—recommended only if you are a very experienced Windows 95 user and have backed up the Registry.

> **CAUTION**   You will not find the Registry Editor on any menu because inexperienced tampering with it could render your computer unusable. You should back up the Registry before any direct editing. (See "Registry: Backing Up.")

Why Use the Registry Editor?

The Registry Editor gives you power to configure Windows 95 features that are available only by editing the Registry. For example, you can create *subkeys* to add sounds for application events, or delete subkeys to remove selected Windows 95 icons from your desktop. Or you may read about other customizations you can make—be careful.

Platinum Edition Using Windows 95, published by Que, describes the Registry in detail and gives several examples of useful changes you can make using the Registry Editor.

Steps

1. Choose Start, Run.

2. Type **regedit** in the Open text box and choose OK. The Registry Editor window opens.

   The left pane shows the hierarchy of keys and subkeys. Open the levels the same way you use Explorer. The right pane shows the values for the selected key or subkey.

3. Locate and edit values only if you know what you are doing. There is no Undo command, or any opportunity to close without saving. Every change is the real thing.

 4. Close the Registry Editor by clicking its Close button. You may have to restart Windows to see the effect of some edits.

Security: Setting Up Passwords

If you work in an environment where you need to secure access to data on your computer, you can require a password before Windows will start.

Steps

 1. Choose Start, Settings, Control Panel, then double-click the Passwords icon. Click the Change Passwords tab.

2. Click the Change Windows Password button to display the Change Windows Password dialog box.

3. Type your old password in the Old Password text box. If you do not currently have a Windows password, leave this text box blank.

4. Type your new password in the New Password and Confirm Password text boxes. Choose OK and then click Close.

To remove a password, type the old password in the Old Password text box and leave the other two text boxes blank.

NOTE If you have network passwords, they are listed when you open the Change Windows Password dialog box. You can change them to match your Windows password. ■

(See also "Customizing: Settings for Each User.")

Sounds: Assigning to System Events

Windows assigns certain sounds to system events, such as starting and exiting Windows, errors, and emptying the Recycle Bin. You can change the sounds and even add your own sound files.

Steps

1. Choose Start, Settings, Control Panel. Double-click the Sounds icon to display the Sounds Properties sheet.

2. In the Events list box, select an event for which you want to assign or change the sound.

3. In the Name drop-down list, select a .WAV file for the event. You can click Details to view properties of the selected .WAV file. If the file you want is not in the list, click Browse, select the file, and click OK. Click the Play button to the right of the Preview icon to hear the sound.

4. In the Schemes drop-down list, you can select an entire sound scheme instead of assigning individual event sounds.

   To save your own selections as a scheme, choose Save As to name the scheme. To delete a scheme, select it and then choose Delete.

5. Click Apply to make the changes and keep the Sounds Properties sheet open to make additional changes. Choose OK to accept the changes and close the sheet.

TIP You can install the following sound schemes in Windows setup, Multimedia component: Jungle, Musica, Robotz, and Utopia. Then you select the scheme in the Sounds Properties sheet.

CUSTOMIZING WINDOWS 95

You can create your own .WAV files if you have a microphone and sound card. (See "Sound: Using Sound Recorder" in the "Multimedia" part of this book.) You can also purchase collections of sounds or find them free on bulletin boards, online services, and the Internet.

TIP   The best place to save a .WAV file for use in Windows applications is in the \Windows\Media folder. This will cause the .WAV file to be displayed on the Name drop-down list in the Sounds Properties sheet.

Start Menu: Adding Items

You can add items to the Start menu to customize it. Add applications to the first level, or to the Programs submenu. You will notice that most Windows 95 applications automatically add the program to the Programs menu, but others, such as Corel WordPerfect Suite 7, appear on the main Start menu.

TIP   Add a program to the top of the Start menu quickly by dragging it from the Explorer or My Computer window and dropping it on the Start button. You can also drag and drop a desktop icon to the Start button to put the shortcut on the Start menu.

Steps

1. Right-click a part of the taskbar where no buttons appear. Choose Properties from the shortcut menu to open the Taskbar Properties sheet. Click the Start Menu Programs tab.

2. Click Add to display the Create Shortcut dialog box. Click Browse to open the Browse dialog box. Select the file—usually with an .EXE extension—for the program you want to add to the Start menu, and then choose Open.

3. The selected path and file should appear in the Command Line text box in the Create Shortcut dialog box.

Choose Next to display the Select Program Folder dialog box.

4. Select the folder location where you want the program to appear. If you want the program to appear at the top of the Start menu, select the Start Menu folder. If you want the program to appear on the Programs menu, select the Programs folder.

5. In the Select a Name for the Shortcut text box, type the words you want to appear on the Start (or Programs) menu. Choose Finish. Choose OK to close the Taskbar Properties sheet.

TIP You can create a new folder on the Start menu by choosing New Folder in the Select Program Folder dialog box.

Start Menu: Removing Items

If you have added items to the Start menu or Programs menu, you can remove them. Some uninstall programs do not remove the application from the menu, so you are left to do the job yourself.

Steps

1. Choose Start, Settings, Taskbar to open the Taskbar Properties sheet. Click the Start Menu Programs tab.

2. Click Remove to display the Remove Shortcuts/Folders dialog box.

3. Select the item(s) you want to remove from the Start menu or Programs menu.

4. Click the Remove button to remove the item(s). Click Close and then click OK to close the Taskbar Properties sheet.

(See also "Removing: Start Menu Shortcuts and Folders" in the "Applications and Accessories" part of this book.)

CUSTOMIZING WINDOWS 95

NOTE The Start menu contains a Documents submenu that shows recently used documents. To clear the items from the Documents menu, display the Taskbar Properties sheet, click the Start Menu Programs tab, and then click the Clear button. Choose either OK or Cancel to close the sheet. (See also "Removing: All Documents from the Document Menu" in the "Applications and Accessories" part of this book.) ■

Start Menu: Reorganizing the Programs Menu

If you have many items on the Programs menu, you may find it helpful to create some general categories that a number of your programs will fit into. You can start by adding a new folder on the Programs menu and then you can move other folders or programs into it.

Steps

1. Right-click the Start button and then click Explore.

2. In the left pane of the Explorer window, click the Programs folder. Choose File, New, Folder. Type a name for the folder that will appear on the Programs menu and then press Enter.

3. Click the + next to the Programs folder. If you want to move an entire folder to the new folder, click the folder you want to move. If you want to move the contents of another folder, click that folder in the left pane to reveal its contents in the right pane.

4. Drag the icons from the right pane into the new folder or other existing folders in the left pane. Repeat Steps 2 and 3 to create additional folders as needed.

5. To delete any extra folders you have emptied, click each folder and then click the Delete button in the toolbar.

Choose Start, Programs to check the appearance of your changes on the actual menu. You can do this while Explorer is still open so that you can continue to move folders.

Taskbar: Changing Options

The Taskbar Properties sheet gives you options of hiding or displaying the taskbar, turning the clock area on or off, and changing the size of the Start menu.

Steps

1. Right-click a part of the taskbar where no buttons appear.

2. Choose Properties to open the Taskbar Properties sheet.

3. Click the Taskbar Options tab. Click any of the check boxes, as described in the following table, to turn the option on or off. Click OK.

Taskbar Properties

Check Box	Description
Always on Top	Taskbar displays over all open windows.
Auto Hide	Hides the taskbar, making more space available on your desktop. The taskbar reappears when you move your mouse pointer to the bottom of the screen (or the current location of the taskbar). The taskbar disappears again when you move the pointer away.
Show Small Icons in Start Menu	Displays the Start menu with smaller icons and no Windows banner, therefore making the menu smaller. The Programs menu is unaffected because it already has smaller icons.
Show Clock	Hides or displays the taskbar clock area that displays the clock and system-related icons.

Taskbar: Moving

The default position for the taskbar is horizontally across the bottom of the screen. You can move the taskbar to the top or to either side of the screen (vertically), too.

CUSTOMIZING WINDOWS 95

Steps

1. Point to a part of the taskbar where no buttons appear.

2. Click with the left mouse button and drag the taskbar to another edge of the screen. You will see a shaded line that indicates the new position of the taskbar.

3. Release the mouse button.

The taskbar is wider—to accommodate the words on the buttons—when placed at the sides of the screen. You can change the width of the taskbar. (See "Taskbar: Resizing.")

Taskbar: Resizing

When your taskbar is positioned horizontally, you may have noticed that the taskbar buttons become smaller when you open many applications. Eventually, you cannot read much of the application names. But if you are willing to give up a little more desktop space, you can change the height of the taskbar to make multiple rows of longer buttons.

If your taskbar is positioned vertically on either side of the screen, the button width may make the taskbar very wide, taking up too much of the desktop. Wherever the taskbar is positioned, you can resize it by following the same steps.

Steps

1. Point to the long edge of the taskbar, where the pointer becomes a double arrow. If the taskbar is at the bottom of the screen, you will point to the upper edge of the taskbar.

2. Click with the left mouse button and drag the edge to the size you want.

3. Release the mouse button.

The horizontal taskbar can only be resized in full button heights. The vertical taskbar can be resized in pixel increments.

TIP You can make the vertical taskbar so narrow that only the application icons show, without words. (If you point to the icons, the button tip pops up to show you its name.) However, you may not be able to read the minutes on the taskbar clock. If you are trying to save desktop space, perhaps you would rather hide the taskbar. (See "Taskbar: Changing Options.")

Taskbar: Using the Taskbar Menu

The taskbar has another menu for rearranging windows on the desktop and accessing the taskbar properties.

Steps

1. Right-click in a blank area of the taskbar to display the shortcut menu.
2. Choose a command from the menu, as described in the following table.

Taskbar Menu Commands

Command	Description
Cascade	Display windows overlapped from left to right, or top to bottom.
Undo Cascade	Return cascaded windows to their previous sizes. (Available only after using Cascade.)
Tile Horizontally	Display windows top to bottom without overlapping.
Tile Vertically	Display windows left to right without overlapping.
Undo Tile	Return windows to their previous sizes. (Available only after a Tile command.)
Minimize All Windows	Reduce all open windows to buttons on the taskbar.
Properties	Display the Taskbar Properties sheet where you can change the taskbar options or the Start menu.

CUSTOMIZING WINDOWS 95

Windows Components: Adding and Removing

You can use the Add/Remove Programs icon in the Control Panel to add or remove the accessories and other components of Windows.

NOTE In the Windows Setup Components list box, a check mark next to an item indicates that the component is already installed on your system. If the check box is gray with a check mark in it, then one or more subcomponents are installed. If there is no check mark, the item is not installed. You can install all or part of the unchecked items and their components. ■

Steps

1. Choose Start, Settings, Control Panel. Double-click the Add/Remove Programs icon and then choose the Windows Setup tab in the Add/Remove Programs Properties sheet.

2. In the Components list box, select a component (click the name, not the check box). The Description box near the bottom of the sheet displays a description and the number of components that are selected.

3. If the component you selected has subcomponents, click the Details button to view the subcomponents.

   Some subcomponents have additional subcomponents that you can view by clicking Details again.

4. Click check boxes next to components or subcomponents that you want to add or remove. Add a check mark to a blank check box to install that item. Clear the check mark from a check box to uninstall that item.

5. Choose OK to confirm changes on subcomponent selections. When you have finished selecting components and subcomponents, choose OK in the Add/ Remove Programs Properties sheet.

   Supply the Windows disks or CD if prompted. You also may be prompted to restart your computer to complete the installation.

TROUBLESHOOTING   When I added new Windows components, some other components were removed. The components that were checked when you opened Windows Setup must remain checked or they will be uninstalled. If you clear the check box, Windows interprets it as a request to remove that component.

CUSTOMIZING WINDOWS 95

Disk and File Management

Hard disks and floppy disks serve the same purpose: They store information you don't want to lose. The differences are that you can take a floppy disk with you and it doesn't hold very much data; a hard disk stays in your computer and some can hold a lot of data.

You want to be able to manage and use your disks effectively and safely. A cluttered hard disk can be as frustrating as a cluttered desk, making it hard to find and easy to lose important information. On a disk, a file is that element that actually stores the information. You may have a file that stores a business letter, your e-mail, or you company's confidential salary information. You need to be able to put these files into groups that make sense, which is why you will find folders on your disks. Folders, which are analogous to DOS directories, hold files or other folders so that you can organize your disk space more efficiently.

Windows 95 has several programs that allow you to view the contents of your disks. These programs will also let you create new folders, move files or folders, copy files or folders, or delete any files or folders you don't need. These programs will also let you move files from disk to disk. In addition, Windows 95 has tools to prepare your disks for information, maintain your disks' integrity, and synchronize files that travel from disk to disk.

Disks: Copying

You can copy the complete contents of a floppy disk onto another disk with a few simple mouse clicks. This is much easier than copying the disk temporarily to your hard drive, and then from your hard drive to the destination disk.

Steps

1. Insert the disk you want to copy into the drive. Start Explorer by choosing Start, Programs, Windows Explorer.

2. Right-click the appropriate drive and choose Copy Disk from the menu. Click the Start button.

3. When prompted, remove the source disk and insert the destination disk. Click the OK button.

Disks: Defragmenting

You create fragments on your hard drive any time you run an application or when you edit, move, copy, or delete a file. Fragmentation is like taking the pieces of a puzzle and storing them in different boxes along with pieces from other puzzles. Unlike humans, the operating system rarely confuses the pieces from different puzzles or loses any puzzle pieces. For humans, however, the more dispersed the pieces are, the longer it takes the operating system to put the puzzle together. So if you notice your system takes longer and longer to open and close files or run applications, you probably need to defragment your system or put all the pieces of the puzzle in one box. (For another disk maintenance utility, see also "Disks: Maintaining with ScanDisk.")

Steps

1. Start the defragment utility by choosing Start, Run. Enter **defrag** into the Open box and click the OK button.

2. Choose the drive you want to have defragmented and click the OK button. The utility will tell you how fragmented your drive is and whether or not you should actually defragment. If you decide you should proceed with defragmentation, click the Start button.

TIP You should close all applications and stop working on the system while the defragment utility is running. *Defragmenting* your drive can take a while, especially if you have a large hard drive or your hard drive is especially fragmented. So, you might want to start the utility and let it run while you are at lunch.

TIP   If you have the Plus! Pak, you can use its system agent to automatically defragment your system on a set schedule.

DISK AND FILE MANAGEMENT

When to Defragment

If you notice that opening files seems to take longer than usual or your hard drive light stays on longer then usual, you may need to defragment your hard drive. When you run the defragment utility, it will tell you the percentage of your drive that is fragmented and suggest whether or not you should run the utility. However, the defragment utility won't advise you to defragment your drive until it is really necessary; if you notice a slowdown, you should defragment your drive even if the utility tells you that you can wait.

Disks: Maintaining with ScanDisk

As you run applications, move files, delete files, or accidentally turn the power off while the system is running, you can introduce disk errors. Remember when you delete a file, the file's name and location are removed from the *File Allocation Table,* but the data is still out there. Sometimes this leftover data or other problems can bog down your hard drive. ScanDisk can locate these problems and correct many of them automatically. (For an additional disk clean-up utility, see "Disks: Defragmenting.")

Steps

1. Start ScanDisk by choosing Start, Run. Enter **ScanDisk** in the Open box and click the OK button.

2. Choose the drive you want to scan. Choose the Standard Testing option button and check the Automatically Fix Errors check box. Click the Start button.

TIP   Performing a thorough scan takes quite a bit of time. You don't really need to do a thorough test unless you are having serious difficulties.

TIP   If you have the Plus! Pak, you can use its system agent to automatically scan your disk for errors on a set schedule.

When to Use ScanDisk

Any time you are having difficulty with your drive you should try running ScanDisk to look for errors. These difficulties could include slow access, failure to open a file, or system hangs when saving or opening a file. Normally, a standard scan will take care of your difficulties. If you suspect serious errors with the physical mechanics of the drive, you can choose a thorough scan. Thorough scans, however, take much longer so allow extra time when performing one.

Disks: Naming with a Volume Label

A volume label is simply a name for the disk. Having labels on your hard drive(s) can be useful because these labels will be shown when you use Explorer. You can change an existing label or give a new disk its first name.

Steps

1. Start Explorer by choosing Start, Programs, Windows Explorer. If you are changing the volume label for a removable disk, be sure to insert the disk into the appropriate drive.

2. Right-click the drive and choose Properties from the menu. Select the General tab and type the desired volume name into the Label box. Click the OK button.

DriveSpace: Adjusting Free Space

DriveSpace is a *disk compression* utility that lets you store more information on a drive. If you've compressed a drive and you need more free space on the drive or its host, you can adjust the free space distribution. See also "DriveSpace: Compressing a Drive."

If your hard drive is larger than 528M and you are using version 4.00.950 B of Windows 95, you should not use DriveSpace because your systems can take advantage of FAT32. (For more information on FAT32 see "DriveSpace: Compressing a Drive.")

Steps

1. Start DriveSpace by choosing Start, Programs, Accessories, System Tools, DriveSpace. Any compressed drive will have Compressed drive shown next to it, as well as an associated host.

2. Select either the compressed drive or the compressed drive's host. Open the Drive menu and choose Adjust Free Space.

3. Drag the slider to change the free space distribution until it is set as you want. Click the OK button and restart your computer when prompted.

Why Adjust Your Free Space?

When you compress a drive you always have the compressed drive itself and a host drive that is not compressed. Free space is distributed between two drives. If you have some system files or other files that cannot be compressed, you need to store them on your host drive. You may need to adjust the free space to allow more room on the host drive to store the incompressible files. By the same token, if you have a file that can be compressed but you are out of room on your compressed drive, you may need to adjust the free space to allow more room on your compressed drive.

DriveSpace: Compressing a Drive

As you add more applications and data to your computer, you may start to run low on free hard drive space. DriveSpace is a *disk compression* utility that comes with Windows 95. It will allow you to compress the information that you store on your hard drive, thus giving you more space on the hard drive. (See also "DriveSpace: Compressing Part of a Disk" and "DriveSpace: Returning to Normal.")

DISK AND FILE MANAGEMENT

If your hard drive is larger than 528M and you are using version 4.00.950 B of Windows 95, you should not use DriveSpace because your system can take advantage of FAT32. Without FAT32, a file that only needs 10 blocks of space may be given 16 because the system allocates space in 8-block chunks. Compression utilities like DriveSpace were able to put more on a hard drive by not wasting unused blocks.

FAT32 is built into version 4.00.950 B, and it already uses the hard drive more effectively by not allocating unused blocks to a file. So, if you have 4.00.950 B and your hard drive is larger than 528M, you should not compress your drive but instead take advantage of FAT32.

Steps

1. Start DriveSpace by choosing Start, Programs, Accessories, System Tools, DriveSpace. Any compressed drive will have Compressed drive shown next to it, as well as an associated host.

2. If you want to compress a drive, select the drive from the Drives on This Computer list. Open the Drive menu and choose Compress. In the Compress dialog box, you can click the Options button to change the host drive letter, the amount of free space on the host drive, and whether or not the host drive should be hidden. Close the Options dialog box by clicking the OK button.

3. Once your options are set, click the Start button. If you haven't already backed up your file, be sure to click the Back Up Files button when prompted. After backing up, click the Compress Now button. Restart the computer when prompted.

CAUTION   Compressing a drive could take several hours, during which time you cannot use your computer.

When to Compress a Drive

If you do not have Windows 95 version 4.00.950 B and you would like to put more on your hard drive, you should consider compressing the drive. DriveSpace allows you to store more on your drive by better allocating the space and applying some compression techniques.

If you are using Windows 95 version 4.00.950 B but your hard drive is less than 528M, you may compress your hard drive. If your hard drive is larger than 528M, however, you should not compress your hard drive, but instead take advantage of FAT32, which basically performs the same function as DriveSpace by better allocating hard drive space.

DriveSpace: Compressing Part of a Disk

Disk compression allows you to store more information on your hard disk; however, you may not want to compress your entire hard disk. DriveSpace allows you to specify a portion of your free hard drive space to use as a compressed disk. (See also "DriveSpace: Compressing a Drive.")

Steps

1. Start DriveSpace by choosing Start, Programs, Accessories, System Tools, DriveSpace. Any compressed drive will have Compressed drive shown next to it, as well as an associated host.

2. Select the uncompressed drive with free space you would like to partially compress. Choose Advanced, Create Empty. You can accept the default drive letter or choose a different drive letter from the drop-down list. In the Using text box, enter the number of megabytes of free space you want used to create the new drive.

3. Check the values displayed in The New Drive Will Contain text box and the Afterwards, Drive text box to make sure they are acceptable. If the values are acceptable, click the Start button.

TIP If you aren't sure how much free space to enter in the Using text box, but you know the amount of Free Space you want the new drive to have, you can enter that value directly into The New Drive Will Contain text box. Windows 95 will automatically calculate the amount of free space needed for the Using text box.

DriveSpace: Returning to Normal

DriveSpace is a *disk compression* utility that lets you store more information on a disk. You can also use DriveSpace to decompress a drive if you need or want the compression removed. This means that previously compressed information is expanded to its original size, so make sure you have enough free space to accommodate the expansion. (See also "DriveSpace: Compressing a Drive.")

Steps

1. Start DriveSpace by choosing Start, Programs, Accessories, System Tools, DriveSpace. Any compressed drive will have Compressed drive shown next to it, as well as an associated host.

2. Select the drive you want to decompress, or return to normal. Choose Drive, Uncompress. Click the Start button.

3. If you haven't backed up your files, click the Back Up Files button. Once your files are backed up, click the Uncompress Now button.

CAUTION   Decompressing a drive could take several hours, during which time you cannot use your computer.

Why Return to Normal?

If you are changing machines or operating systems and you need to format your drive, you must decompress the drive before you can format it. In addition, if you decide you really don't need the extra space given with disk compression, you should consider decompressing the drive to reduce the compression overhead when reading and writing to the drive.

DriveSpace: Viewing Properties of a Compressed Drive

If you've compressed a drive and you want to see how much free space is available, the compression ratio, or other information, you can view the drive's properties. (See also "DriveSpace: Compressing a Drive.")

Steps

1. Start DriveSpace by choosing Start, Programs, Accessories, System Tools, DriveSpace. Any compressed drive will have Compressed drive shown next to it, as well as an associated host.

2. Select the drive you want to check. Choose Drive, Properties. The only change you can make is whether or not the host drive is hidden. After viewing or changing the Hide Host Drive option, click the OK button.

File Types: Changing the Icon

Windows 95 uses the extension, any character after the last period of a file name, to determine a file's file type. This file type in turn is associated with an icon that will be shown whenever files of that type are listed in Explorer. If you don't like a particular file type icon, you can easily choose another icon. (See also "File Types: Displaying or Hiding," "File Types: Editing," "File Types: Registering," and "File Types: Removing.")

Steps

1. Start Explorer by choosing Start, Programs, Windows Explorer. Choose View, Options.

2. Select the File Types tab. Choose the file type you want to change from the Registered File Types list and click the Edit button.

3. Click the Change Icon button. Enter the name of the file that contains the icon into the File Name box; or click the Browse button, select the file, and click Open. If the file has more than one icon, select the appropriate icon in the Current Icon box, and then click the OK or Close button until you return to Explorer.

TIP Windows 95 has several files that have a selection of fun icons to choose from. In the Windows folder enter **MORICONS .DLL** or **PROGMAN.EXE** for file name, and you can choose from many standard application and fun icons. In the Windows\System folder, enter **PIFMGR.DLL** for file name and you can choose some colorful, fun icons.

File Types: Displaying or Hiding

Windows 95 uses the characters in the extension of a file name to determine a file's file type. Windows 95 has the ability to hide files that are of a certain type. The types of files it hides are typically system files. Because you don't want to accidentally delete or change a system file, hiding them can be a good idea. You may, however, need to edit a system file so you should know how to unhide the files. (See also "File Types: Changing the Icon," "File Types: Editing," "File Types: Registering," and "File Types: Removing.")

Steps

1. Start Explorer by choosing Start, Programs, Windows Explorer. Choose View, Options.

2. Click the View tab and choose Show All Files if you want to see hidden files, or choose Hide Files of These Types if you don't want certain files displayed.

File Types: Editing

Windows 95 uses the characters in the extension of a file name to determine a file's file type. This file type in turn is associated with an icon, an application, and other key features that determine how the file is handled by Windows. If you want to change a file type's behavior, you need to edit its registration. (See also "File Types: Changing the Icon," "File Types: Displaying or Hiding," "File Types: Registering," and "File Types: Removing.")

Steps

1. Start Windows Explorer by choosing Start, Programs, Windows Explorer. Choose View, Options.

2. Select the File Types tab. Choose the file type you want to change from the Registered File Types list and click the Edit button.

3. Make the desired changes and then click the OK button until you return to Explorer.

Why Edit a File Type?

If you don't like the application that opens when you double-click certain files, or you don't like the icon a certain file type uses, you need to know how to edit the file type's registration. You can choose a different application or even define a list of applications you would like to choose from. For example, you could create an action for a .TXT file that would open the selected file in Notepad, and another action that would open a .TXT file in Wordpad. Both actions would be available anytime you right-click a .TXT file, and you could choose the action you want.

File Types: Registering

Windows 95 uses the characters in the extension of a file name to determine a file's file type. If you have files with an extension that has not been registered, you can register it through Explorer. Here you can choose the associated application, icon, even a description of the file type. (See also "File Types: Changing the Icon," "File Types: Displaying or Hiding," "File Types: Editing," and "File Types: Removing.")

Steps

1. Start Explorer by choosing Start, Programs, Windows Explorer. Choose View, Options.

2. Select the File Type tab and click the New Type button.

3. Enter a comment about the file type in the Description text box, the file type's extension in the Associated Extension text box, and the file type's *MIME* information, if applicable.

4. Click the New Button under the Actions list. Enter a name like **open** or **run** into the Action box. Enter the path, program, and switches you want to use to perform this action into the Application Used box, or click the Browse button and select the application. Click the OK button until you return to Explorer.

NOTE You can have more than one action for any particular extension. These actions will all be displayed when you right-click a file of the registered type. The action that will be performed when you double-click the file is the default action. The default action will be bolded in the Actions list when you edit the file type. You can change the default action by selecting the new default action in the Action list and clicking the Set Default button. ▦

Why Register a File Type?

As you use Explorer to browse files and folders, you will notice that some files have specific icons. These icons let you know what type the file is. File type determines more than just the icon, it also determines the description you see if you look at the file's details and the application that will be used to open the file. An application usually registers its file types. If, however, you create files with custom or special extensions (such as the author's initials) you need to register these special extensions as a file.

File Types: Removing

Windows 95 uses the characters in the extension of a file name to determine a file's file type. If you have file types registered that don't even exist on your system, or you want to delete the current registration and start again, you can remove the file type from Windows 95. (See also "File Types: Changing the Icon," "File Types: Displaying or Hiding," "File Types: Editing," and "File Types: Registering.")

Steps

1. Start Explorer by choosing Start, Programs, Windows Explorer. Choose View, Options.

2. Select the File Types tab. Choose the file type you want to remove from the Registered File Types list and click the Remove button.

Files: Finding

Locating a file can be difficult, especially if you have a large drive or several drives. Explorer includes a Find utility to search through a drive for you. (See also the "Files and Folders" sections, the "Files" sections, and the "Folders" sections.)

Steps

1. Start Explorer by choosing Start, Programs, Windows Explorer. Select the drive you want to search or the drive and folder you want to search.

2. Choose Tools, Find, then choose Files or Folders.

3. Enter the name of the file or folder you want and click the Find Now button. A box will appear with any matching files or folders displayed. You can open, move, copy, or delete a file from this display box.

 TIP You can use the DOS wild card characters when performing searches with the Find utility. Use * in place of 0 or multiple characters, and ? in place of a single character.

Files: Managing with My Computer

My Computer is another file management tool similar to Explorer that contains your hard drive(s), mapped network drives, peripheral drives, Control Panel, and the Printer Folder. You can easily access almost all of your resources from My Computer.

Steps

1. Start My Computer by double-clicking its icon on the desktop.

2. You can open any drive or folder by double-clicking its icon. To return to the previous location, press the Backspace key.

3. You can move, copy, rename, or delete any file or folder in My Computer using the same steps described in the previous tasks such as "Files and Folders: Moving and Coping," "Files and Folders: Deleting," or "Files and Folders: Renaming." My Computer works like Windows Explorer except that it only shows the Contents pane.

 TIP If you find the multiple windows that My Computer opens annoying and messy, you'll want to change your browse option. In My Computer, choose View, Options. Select the Folder tab and choose the option Browse Folders by Using a Single Window. Click the OK button.

Files: Previewing with Quick View

If you are looking for a particular file but you don't know its name, you can take advantage of Quick View. Quick View will let you see the contents of a file, but you don't have to wait for the associated application to start. (See also "File Types: Registering" and "Files and Folders: Viewing with Explorer.")

Steps

1. Start Explorer by choosing Start, Programs, Windows Explorer.

2. Locate the file you want to preview. Right-click the file's icon and choose Quick View.

3. This will start the viewer. You can look at the contents of the file and if it is a file you want to edit, click the associated application icon on the left side of the toolbar.

4. After you are done viewing the file, click the Close button on the right-hand side of the title bar.

DISK AND FILE MANAGEMENT

TROUBLESHOOTING **When I right-click a file, I don't have a Quick View option.** You need to add Quick View to your system. Open the Control Panel by choosing Start, Settings, Control Panel. Double-click the Add/Remove Programs icon and select the Windows Setup tab. Select Accessories from the Components list and click the Details button. Check the Quick View check box and click the OK button until you return to the Control Panel. If the Quick View option is not immediately available, restart your computer.

Why Use Quick View?

Quick View is a handy utility if you are looking for a file among many files but you don't remember the file's name. Some applications may take quite a while to start and open a file. If you use Quick View, you can quickly scan the contents of each file until you find the file you need.

Files: Protecting from Viruses

Viruses are programs that harm your computer in some fashion. Some are more annoying than harmful, but others can destroy the contents of your computer system and render it useless. You can protect yourself from viruses by being careful about what you put on your machine and running anti-virus software regularly. (See also "MS Backup: Backing Up Files.")

Steps

1. You can protect your machine from viruses by performing each of the following tasks.

* Install anti-virus software according to the directions included with the software. Run the program regularly.

Update the software periodically according to instructions included with the software.

* Only accept or purchase software from known vendors.

* If you download files from the Internet, create a special download folder and have the anti-virus software scan the folder each time you download any new files.

When to Scan for Viruses

If you have a completely closed system—you never put new software on, you copy files from a floppy, or you never communicate with other devices—then you don't need a virus checker. Because this is rarely the situation, you should add a virus checker to your start-up folder. This will check your system for viruses each time your system is booted. In addition, if you download files from the Internet or other online services, make sure you download them to a separate directory and scan all files before using them on your system.

Files: Restoring Deleted

If you delete a file and later decide you made a mistake, you are in luck. Windows 95 will store deleted files in its Recycle Bin for a period of time. As long as you have recently deleted the file, it should still be in the Recycle Bin. (See also "Files: Deleting" and "MS Backup: Backing Up Files.")

WARNING By default, the Recycle Bin will consume no more than 10 percent of your hard disk space. After the Recycle Bin reaches its size limit, it starts removing files permanently from your hard drive. The oldest files, based on deletion date not creation date, in the Recycle Bin will be deleted first. This is not usually a problem unless you delete a large number of files at one time. If you delete more than 10 percent of your hard drive (or whatever the size limit is) you will not be able to restore all the files.

Steps

1. Open the Recycle Bin by double-clicking its icon on the desktop.
2. Locate the file or folder you want to restore. Right-click the item's icon and choose Restore from the menu.

Files: Synchronizing with Windows Briefcase

If you take files back and forth between PCs you probably get tired of figuring out where the most current files are located.

With Windows 95's Briefcase, you simply pop the files from your primary machine into the Briefcase, work from your Briefcase when you are at another machine, then copy the Briefcase back to your machine when you return. You no longer have to check file dates and sizes to keep track. (See also "Files and Folders: Moving and Copying" and "Files and Folders: Viewing with Explorer.")

Steps

1. If you do not have a Briefcase icon on your desktop, create one by right-clicking any open desktop space, and choosing New, Briefcase from the menu.

2. Start Explorer by choosing Start, Programs, Windows Explorer. Open the folder that contains the files you want to put in your Briefcase. Drag the files from My Computer and drop them on the Briefcase icon. Drag the Briefcase icon from the desktop and drop it onto the floppy drive in Explorer. (The desktop icon won't disappear.)

3. Now insert the floppy in your secondary machine, portable, or whichever machine you want the files synchronized on. Use the files directly from the briefcase, opening and saving them directly from the briefcase.

4. When you return to your main machine, insert the floppy disk into the drive. Start Explorer and open the floppy drive. Drag the Briefcase icon in the floppy drive and drop it on the Briefcase on the desktop. Windows 95 will take care of synchronizing your files so that you are always using the current version.

TROUBLESHOOTING **When I right-click the desktop and choose New, I don't have a Briefcase.** You need to add Briefcase to your system. Open the Control Panel by choosing Start, Settings, Control Panel. Double-click the Add/Remove Programs icon and select the Windows Setup tab. In the Components list, check the Briefcase check box and click the OK button until you return to the Control Panel.

Why Use Briefcase?

If you consistently use more than one computer to edit the same file, you'll find the Briefcase is a handy utility. You don't have to worry about which machine has the most current copies of your work or about overwriting recent changes.

Files: Working with Long File Names

Before Windows 95 you probably had to deal with file names that could only have an eight-character name and a three-letter extension. That is, you used the 8.3 convention. With Windows 95, you can have long file names with spaces, multiple periods, and even long extensions. (See also "File and Folders: Renaming.")

Steps

1. When naming a file, use up to 256 characters, numbers, spaces, or symbols except for / \ ; ? " < > * : or |. Windows 95 will automatically truncate the file name if used with an older application that doesn't support long file names.

2. Make sure the file name combined with the folder name does not exceed 256 total characters.

> **CAUTION** Although Windows 95 can automatically truncate long file names, older versions of Windows or DOS may not be able to use files with long names. So, if you exchange files with someone running an older operating system, you will need to stick to the previous 8.3 naming convention.

Files and Folders: Changing Properties

Files and folders have properties associated with them like read-only, write, hidden, and others. You can view the properties of a file or a folder and then change them to suit your needs. (See also "Files and Folders: Deleting," "Files and Folders: Moving and Copying," "Files and Folders: Renaming," and "Files and Folders: Viewing with Explorer.")

Steps

1. Start Explorer by choosing Start, Programs, Windows Explorer.

2. Select the file or folder you want to change and right-click its icon. Choose Properties from the menu.

3. Make the desired changes and click the OK button until you return to Explorer.

When to Change Properties

If you have a file that you want to edit but you can't because it is read-only, you need to change that file's properties. In addition, on a network you can use properties to share your files with other network users. Before sharing a file, you will probably want to change its properties to read-only. (For more information on sharing see "Sharing: Files on a Network" in the "Networking" part of this book.)

Files and Folders: Deleting

Because disk space is a resource you don't want to waste, you should delete files and folders you no longer need. (See also "Files and Folders: Changing Properties," "Files and Folders: Moving and Copying," "Files and Folders: Renaming," "Files and Folders: Viewing with Explorer," and "MS Backup: Backing Up Files.")

Steps

1. Start Explorer by choosing Start, Programs, Windows Explorer.

2. Select the file or folder you want to delete and press the Delete key or click the Delete tool.

Files and Folders: Moving and Copying

Hard drives and disks are like dresser drawers; they can become cluttered and confusing. If you start finding your sock "files" in your T-shirt drawer, you might consider moving or copying the files into their correct location. (See also "Files and Folders: Changing Properties," "Files and Folders:

DISK AND FILE MANAGEMENT

Deleting," "Files and Folders: Renaming," "Files and Folders: Viewing with Explorer," and "MS Backup: Backing Up Files.")

Steps

1. Start Explorer by choosing Start, Programs, Windows Explorer.

2. Select the file or folder you want to move or copy. Right-click the icon of the folder or file. If you want to move the file or folder choose Cut; if you want to copy the file or folder choose Copy.

3. Select the new location for the file. Right-click in some open space in the Content's pane of the location. Choose Paste from the menu.

When to Move versus When to Copy

Moving and Copying files are two very different actions. If you move a file, you are deleting it from its original location. If you are simply reorganizing your hard drive, moving files from one location to another is usually fine. If you want to put a file on a floppy or network drive, you probably want to copy the file so that you still have it on your local computer.

Files and Folders: Renaming

File and folder names should always describe the contents of the file or folder. Sometimes, however, the contents may change, or the file or folder may contain a revision number that needs updating. If you have a file or folder with a name that just isn't right, you should rename it. (See also "Files and Folders: Changing Properties," "Files and Folders: Deleting," "Files and Folders: Moving and Copying," and "Files and Folders: Viewing with Explorer.")

Steps

1. Start Explorer by choosing Start, Programs, Windows Explorer.

2. Locate the file or folder you want to rename. (See "Files and Folders: Viewing with Explorer.") Right-click the file or folder icon, choose Rename from the menu, and enter the new name.

TIP   You can also quickly start Explorer by right-clicking the My
Computer icon on the desktop. From the pop-up menu choose
Explore.

Files and Folders: Viewing Options

You can use Explorer to group and sort your files and folders,
as well as provide or hide file information. You can also choose
to have large or small icons or several useful options. (See also
"Files and Folders: Viewing with Explorer.")

Steps

1. Start Explorer by choosing Start, Programs, Windows,
   Explorer. Double-click the drive and then the folder you
   want to view.

2. Open the View menu. You can first choose whether or
   not to display the Toolbar or the Status Bar. If a check
   mark is next to the item, it will be displayed; if a check
   mark is not next to the item, it will not be displayed.
   To check or uncheck an item, simply click Toolbar or
   Status Bar.

   The toolbar is a horizontal bar under the menu that
   contains buttons. Each button on the toolbar performs
   an action you can normally do from a menu. These
   buttons are handy because they only require one click,
   whereas choosing a menu option may require several
   clicks.

   The status bar is a horizontal bar at the very bottom
   of the window. It displays information about current
   selections or actions. For each, if you select a file, the
   status bar will display the file size.

3. Next, you can change how the files and folders are
   displayed in the right pane or the Contents pane. You can
   choose one of the four options: Large Icons, Small Icons,
   List, or Details by clicking the option you want.

   Large Icons will show each file/folder as an icon about
   the size of your desktop icons. Small Icons will show

each file about the size of the icon that normally appears on the upper-left side of the title bar. For both large and small icons, the files/folders are arranged in order (see the next step) from left to right in horizontal rows.

List will display the files/folders as small icons, but instead of ordering the files/folders from left to right, the files/folders are ordered from top to bottom in vertical columns.

Details will display the files/folders as small icons in a single, vertical column. Beside each icon will be columns of information about the file/folder such as size, file type, file date, and modification date.

4. You should also determine in what order you want your icons arranged. From the View menu choose Arrange Icons. You will be given four options: By Name, By Type, By Size, or By Date.

If you choose By Name, the files will be arranged alphabetically by file name. If you choose By Type, the icons will first be grouped with files of the same type and arranged alphabetically within each group. If you choose By Date, the files will be arranged in order from the most recent to oldest. If you choose By Size, the files will be ordered by file size with the smallest file being the first.

For small and large icons, the Arrange Icons menu will also let you check the Auto Arrange icon which will force all icons into strict rows and columns so you cannot have an icon out of line. If you choose not to check this option, and your icons become messy, you can realign them. Open the View menu and choose Line Up Icons.

5. If you have moved, copied, or deleted some files and folders but don't see the changes, you can update the Explorer Contents page. Choose View, Refresh or press the F5 key.

Files and Folders: Viewing with Explorer

Explorer is the Windows 95 file management tool. You can use Explorer to see the contents of various drives, folders, and files. (See also "Files and Folders: Changing Properties," "Files and Folders: Deleting," "Files and Folders: Moving and Copying," "Files and Folders: Renaming," and "Files and Folders: Viewing Options.")

Steps

1. Start Explorer by choosing Start, Programs, Windows Explorer.

2. Locate the file or folder you want to view and double-click its icon. The folder will be displayed in the Contents pane of Explorer. The file will be displayed in the application specified in the file type's registration. (See also "File Types: Registering" for more information.)

Folders: Creating

Folders act as drawers on a hard drive to hold other folders or files. They let you organize your hard drive by putting common files or folders together. You can use Windows Explorer to create new folders. (See also "Files and Folders: Changing Properties," "Files and Folders: Deleting," "Files and Folders: Moving and Copying," "Files and Folders: Renaming," and "Files and Folders: Viewing Options.")

Steps

1. Start Explorer by choosing Start, Programs, Windows Explorer.

2. Double-click the icon of the drive or folder under which you want your new folder to appear.

3. Choose File, New, Folder. Enter a name for your folder. A new, empty folder appears. You then can drag files into this new folder. For information on how to rename the folder see "Files and Folders: Renaming." If you created the folder in the wrong location, see "Files and Folders: Moving and Copying" or "Files and Folders: Deleting."

DISK AND FILE MANAGEMENT

Formatting: Floppy Disks

Floppy disks are great for taking a file home or across town, as well as just storing important files in a second location. Before you can put anything on that floppy, however, you need to format it to hold data. See also "Formatting: Hard Drives," "Disks: Copying," and "Disks: Naming with a Volume Label."

Steps

1. Insert the disk into the appropriate drive. Start Explorer by choosing Start, Programs, Windows Explorer.

2. Right-click the applicable drive and choose Format. Set the desired options including a label if desired. Click the Start button. Windows 95 will format your floppy and display the results in a dialog box when complete.

> **WARNING**   Formatting a previously formatted disk will destroy any files previously stored on the disk. Be sure the floppy doesn't contain anything you need before you format it.

When to Format a Floppy Disk

If you have a new disk that is not preformatted, you must format it before you can store any information on it. In addition, if you have a disk that you had a lot of information stored on and now you want to put all new information on it, you may want to format the disk to thoroughly clean off the old files and prepare the disk for the new information.

Formatting: Hard Drives

Hard drives are permanent storage devices for your data and applications. If you run out of hard drive space and you want to add a new hard drive, you must format that drive before you can use it. See also "Formatting: Floppy Disks," "Disks: Defragmenting," "Disks: Maintaining with Scan Disk," and "Disks: Naming with a Volume Label."

Steps

1. If you are installing a new hard drive, insert the Windows 95 startup disk into drive A: and power on the computer. Windows will detect the new drive and ask you if you want to allocate all of the unallocated space on your drive. Answer yes.

2. You can also format an uncompressed drive from Windows. First, make sure you have backed up important files. (See the "MS Backup" sections for more information.) Make sure all applications are closed, then start Explorer by choosing Start, Programs, Windows Explorer. Right-click the drive you want to format and choose Format from the menu. Set the options and if desired, enter a label, then click the Start button.

WARNING You cannot format the drive that contains Windows while Windows is running. If you need to format this drive, you need a disk copy of MS-DOS with the Format command, or a set of Windows 95 upgrade disks that contains a disk for formatting disks. Formatting the drive that contains Windows will make your system unbootable without a boot floppy. Before proceeding with the format, make sure you can boot your system from the DOS disks or the upgrade disks.

NOTE If your disk was previously compressed, you must decompress it before you can format it. (See also "DriveSpace: Returning to Normal.")

When to Format a Hard Disk

You shouldn't find yourself formatting a hard disk very often. If, however, you have purchased a new hard drive or an additional hard drive, you need to format the drive before you can store information on it. Sometimes, if a drive and operating system become very corrupted, you may have to format your existing drive and start from scratch. Before formatting your existing drive, however, back up your files and make sure you have a Startup disk with the Format utility.

DISK AND FILE MANAGEMENT

MS Backup: Backing Up File Sets

MS Backup is an application that facilitates the archival of important files on you computer. Even if you've never had a hard drive fail or become corrupted, your should always make regular backup copies of your critical files. MS Backup allows you to create file sets that you can backup regularly. (See also "MS Backup: Creating File Sets," "MS Backup: Installing," "MS Backup: Changing Settings," and "MS Backup: Restoring Files.")

Steps

1. Start MS Backup by choosing Start, Programs, Accessories, System Tools, Backup. Select the Backup tab.

2. Choose File, Open File Set. Locate and select the file set you want to back up and click the Open button.

3. MS Backup may take several minutes to copy the chosen file set. Once the files have all been copied, click the Next Step button.

4. Select the backup destination and click the Start Backup button. All the files selected in the file set will be copied to the backup destination.

MS Backup: Backing Up Files

Before proceeding with this task, see "MS Backup: Restoring Files" for important information before starting this task. MS Backup is a utility that helps you store important files in the event of a hard drive crash. Even if you've never had a hard drive fail or become corrupted, you should always make regular backup copies of your critical files. (See also "MS Backup: Backing Up File Sets," "MS Backup: Creating File Sets," and "MS Backup: Installing.")

Steps

1. Start MS Backup by choosing Start, Programs, System Tools, Backup. Click the Backup tab.

2. Select the drive with the files you want backed up. To backup an entire drive, click the check box next to the drive in the left pane.

3. If you aren't backing up an entire drive, select the files and folders you want backed up by checking the box next to the file or folder.

4. Click the Next Step button, then select a destination for the backup files. If this is a set of files you will need to back up often, for instructions see "MS-Backup: Creating File Sets" and "MS Backup: Backing Up File Sets."

5. Click the Start Backup button. When prompted, supply a label for the backup set and click the Password Protect button if you want to set a password. Click the OK button until the process is complete and you return to MS Backup.

 TIP When labeling the backup set, you should try to include the date so that you know how old the backed up files are.

When to Back Up Files

How often you need to back up your files depends on how often the files change and how critical the changes are. For many users, once a month is often enough. If your system crashes, you'll lose some information but nothing you can't reproduce with a little time. However, if you store critical information that changes rapidly you should consider backing up more regularly.

MS Backup: Changing Settings

MS Backup is an application that facilitates the archival of important files on you computer. MS Backup will let you view and change its settings to fit your needs. (See also "MS Backup: Installing.")

Steps

1. Start MS Backup by choosing Start, Programs, Accessories, System Tools, Backup.

2. Choose Settings, Options. Select the Backup tab. Select or check the options you want to set and click the OK button.

MS Backup: Creating File Sets

MS Backup is an application that facilitates the archival of important files on you computer. Even if you've never had a hard drive fail or become corrupted, you should always make regular backup copies of your critical files. MS Backup lets you create sets of the files you commonly back up so that you don't have to select the files individually each time. (See also "MS Backup: Backing Up File Sets," "MS Backup: Restoring Files," "MS Backup: Changing Settings," and "MS Backup: Installing.")

Steps

1. Start MS Backup by choosing Start, Programs, Accessories, System Tools, Backup. Select the Backup tab.

2. Select the files you want in the set by clicking the check box next to each desired file. Then click the Next Step button.

3. Select the destination of the backed up files from the Select a Destination list.

4. Choose File, Save As. Enter a name for the backup file set in the File Name box and click the Save button.

5. If you want to continue and back up the file set, click the Start Backup button.

MS Backup: Erasing and Formatting Tapes

Tapes are a handy way to store large chunks of information you don't use regularly. For this reason they are great for backing up systems. MS Backup accounts for tape popularity by automatically detecting a tape backup system and providing some tape maintenance tools. (See also "MS Backup: Installing," "MS Backup: Backing Up File Sets," "MS Backup: Changing Settings," "MS Backup: Backing Up Files," and "MS Backup: Restoring Files.")

Steps

1. Insert a tape into the tape drive. Start MS Backup by choosing Start, Programs, Accessories, System Tools, Backup.

2. If you want to format a tape, choose Tools, Format Tape. Enter a name for the tape and click OK. If this command is grayed out, choose the Redetect Tape command and repeat the step. If the Redetect Tape command is also grayed out, you need to refer to your tape literature or contact your vendor to ensure your tape is properly installed.

3. If you want to erase a tape, choose Tools, Erase Tape. Confirm that you want the tape erased when prompted by clicking the Yes button. If this command is grayed out, choose the Redetect Tape command and repeat the step.

MS Backup: Installing

MS Backup is an application that facilitates the archival of important files on your computer. Even if you've never had a hard drive fail or become corrupted, you should always make regular backup copies of your critical files. If you aren't already using MS Backup or another backup software, you should install MS Backup now. (See also "MS Backup: Backing Up File Sets," "MS Backup: Backing Up Files," "MS Backup: Restoring Files," and "MS Backup: Verifying Files.")

Steps

1. Start the Control Panel by choosing Start, Settings, Control Panel. Double-click the Add/Remove Programs icon.

2. Select the Windows Setup tab. Choose Disk Tools from the list of components and click the Details button.

3. Check the Backup box and click the OK button until you return to the Control Panel.

NOTE You may need to insert your Windows 95 CD or disk(s) to complete the installation. ▪

Why Install MS Backup?

MS Backup is a utility that helps you archive important files. If your system crashes and you cannot retrieve any data from your hard drive, you can restore your important files from your backup copies. This can save you valuable time and resources.

MS Backup: Restoring Files

(See also "MS Backup: Backing Up Files" for more information before proceeding with this task.) MS Backup is an application that facilitates the archival of important files on your computer. You should always make regular backup copies of your critical files. If your hard drive fails or a critical file gets corrupted, you can use MS Backup to restore the file. (See also "MS Backup: Backing Up File Sets" and "MS Backup: Installing.")

Steps

1. Start MS Backup by choosing Start, Programs, Accessories, System Tools, Backup.
2. Select the Restore tab. In the left pane, select the drive that contains the backup files.
3. In the right pane, select the set that contains the files you want restored, and click the Next Step button.
4. Select the folders or files you want restored and click the Restore button. Click the OK button when restoration is complete.

MS Backup: Verifying Files

You can use MS Backup to verify that a file backup and the file on your system are the same. This can be handy if the backup process takes some time and you don't think you've made any changes to a file since your last backup. (See also "MS Backup: Backing Up File Sets" and "MS Backup: Backing Up Files.")

Steps

1. Start MS Backup by choosing Start, Programs, Accessories, System Tools, Backup. Select the Compare tab.
2. In the left pane, select the device that contains the backup files you want to compare. In the right pane, select the backup set containing the files you want to compare.

3. Click the Next Step button. Select the files or folders you want to compare with the original files.

4. Click the Start Compare button. The results will be displayed in the Compare message box. If an error is detected, a dialog box will appear asking you if you would like to review the error. If you do want to review the error click Yes to open the error.log file in Notepad. When you are through checking the results, click the OK button.

When to Verify Files

If your backup process is lengthy, checking to see what files have actually changed since your last backup can save you time. If a file hasn't changed since your last backup, you don't need to waste time backing that file up again.

System: Monitoring

You can monitor the performance of your computer's system components. This can be useful if you're evaluating new hardware or software and you want to know how much of the system resources the new items use. You can also use the System Monitor at any time to check the computer's current performance. (See also "System: Viewing Resources.")

Steps

1. Start the System Monitor by choosing Start, Programs, Accessories, System Tools, System Monitor.

2. The monitor will automatically show you processor usage. If you want to monitor other system items, choose Edit, Add Item or click the Add tool. Select the category of the item from the Category list, then select the item from the Item list. Click the OK button.

3. If you want to remove an item from the Monitor list, choose Edit, Remove Item or click the Remove tool. Select the item you want removed and click OK.

4. To change the color or scale for an item being monitored, choose Edit, Edit Item, or click the Edit tool.

Select the item you want to edit and click OK. If you want to change the color, click the Change button, choose a new color, and click OK.

If you want to control the maximum value of the y-axis, then in the Scale box choose Value and enter the value in the text box. Otherwise, leave the scale set to Automatic and let Windows set the scale.

5. You can choose how the items are displayed by choosing View, Line Charts, Bar Charts, or Numeric charts; you can also click the appropriate tool on the toolbar.

   If you want the charts updated more or less frequently, choose Options, Chart. Move the slider until the update interval is correct, and click the OK button.

TROUBLESHOOTING   I don't have a System Monitor. You need to add System Monitor to your system. Open the Control Panel by choosing Start, Settings, Control Panel. Double-click the Add/Remove Programs icon and select the Windows Setup tab. Select Accessories from the Components list and click the Details button. Check the System Monitor check box and click OK until you return to the Control Panel.

When to Monitor the System

Monitoring your system can be interesting, but it can also be useful. If you are having problems with your system locking up or slowing down, you can use the monitor to tell you what device is using resources when the problems occur. In addition, the monitor can help you determine how many resources an application or process uses. This is great if you are evaluating software and want to know which one uses the resources most effectively.

System: Using Virtual Memory

As you run multiple applications and open multiple files, you are bound to run low on real memory. You can buy more RAM to put in your machine, but soon you'll probably be running low again. A simpler solution is to use virtual memory. When

Windows runs out of RAM for applications or data, it can use your hard drive like RAM. In fact, Windows will configure itself to do this automatically. If, however, you think you need more or less virtual memory than Windows is allowing, you can change the settings. (See also "System: Monitoring" and "System: Viewing Resources.")

Steps

1. Open the Control Panel by choosing Start, Settings, Control Panel. Double-click the System icon and choose the Performance tab.

2. Click the Virtual Memory button. Select the Let Me Specify My Own Virtual Memory Settings option button.

3. Choose the hard disk you want for virtual memory from the Hard Disk list. Specify the Minimum and Maximum number of megabytes you want Windows to use for virtual memory. Click the OK button.

WARNING   You can also choose to disable virtual memory, but this could prevent your computer from running certain applications or opening large files.

WARNING   The hard disk you specify for virtual memory must have at least as much free space as the maximum amount of virtual memory you set. If you are low on hard disk space, a large virtual memory space can cause problems such as not enough space to save or copy a file.

When to Change Virtual Memory Settings

In general, you should let the operating system determine how to best manage virtual memory because Windows 95 is built to use it as efficiently as possible. If, however, you are running low on hard drive space, you can decrease the amount of hard drive used for virtual memory and give yourself more storage room. If you limit the amount of space for virtual memory, however, be prepared to limit how many applications and files you can open at one time.

System: Viewing Resources

You can monitor and check the performance of system components on your computer. This can be useful if you are evaluating new hardware or software and you want to know how much of the system resources the new items use. You can also simply monitor the performance of your system overall. (See also "System: Monitoring.")

Steps

1. For a view of the system's available resources and current settings, open the Control Panel by choosing Start, Settings, Control Panel. Double-click the System icon.

2. Select the Performance tab and you can check what percentage of resources are free, as well as other information.

   For a continual update on system resource use, you can use the System Monitor. (See also "System: Monitoring.")

Printing

 Printing in Microsoft Windows can be as simple as clicking an application's Print button or dragging a document to a printer icon on the desktop. But first you must correctly set up the printer's properties. This section tells you how to install, delete, and configure the printer and its port. Adding a printer in Windows 95 is simplified with the use of the Add Printer Wizard. You make a few selections and Windows gives your printer a default configuration that you can customize later as required.

In both Windows and MS-DOS applications, you can control *print jobs*, watch the status of each queued document in the Print Manager, and if needed, pause or cancel jobs before they print.

Device Manager: Configuring the Printer Port

The Device Manager page of the System Properties sheet identifies the printer's port settings and its conflicts with other hardware. If the printer is not working or is changed to a different port, you need to check the configuration options.

Steps

1. Choose Start, Settings, Control Panel. Double-click the System icon and then choose the Device Manager tab of the System Properties sheet.

2. Double-click the Ports icon. Select the printer port you want to configure—possibly LPT1.

3. Click Properties and then click the Driver tab. Click the Update Driver button to start the Update Device Driver Wizard. If you are configuring LPT1 as a printer port, select No and then click Next.

If you do not see an Update Driver button on the Driver page, refer to the Notes following these steps.

4. In the Models list, select Printer Port, and then click Finish. You may be prompted to insert a Windows 95 disk or CD-ROM.

5. Click the Resources tab. If a conflict is listed in the Conflicting Device list, uncheck the Use Automatic Settings box and then try other settings in the Setting Based On drop-down list. When you find a setting that displays no conflicts, choose OK.

NOTE These steps are based on Microsoft Windows 95, version 4.00.950 A. If your version of Windows 95 is different, your steps for this task will vary. To check your version of Windows, right-click the My Computer icon, choose Properties, and look at the System entry on the General page. ▓

NOTE If your version of Windows displays a Driver Files list box on the Driver page (see previous Steps 3 and 4), the driver file listed in the Driver Files list box should show the most current printer driver available. A .VXD extension signifies a 32-bit virtual driver. If you have a driver with a .DRV extension, you should check with your printer manufacturer to obtain the 32-bit version. Click the Change Driver button and then select a driver from the Models list box, or choose Have Disk to install a driver from a vendor-supplied disk. ▓

Drag and Drop: Creating a Desktop Printer Icon

Windows 95 permits printing from the desktop, which requires that you first create a shortcut icon for the printer on the desktop.

Steps

1. Choose Start, Settings, Printers to open the Printers folder.

2. Select the printer, drag it onto the desktop, and drop it.

3. Click Yes when Windows asks if you want to create a shortcut.

TIP You can open the Printers folder by double-clicking the printer icon in the Control Panel window.

(See also "Copying and Moving: Drag and Drop" in the "Applications and Accessories" part of this book.)

Drag and Drop: Printing from the Desktop

You can print a document in Windows 95 without first starting the application for the document you want to print. You must first have a desktop shortcut for the printer. (See also "Drag and Drop: Creating a Desktop Printer Icon.")

Steps

1. In My Computer, open a folder that contains a printable document and select that document.

2. Drag the document's icon to a printer shortcut icon on the desktop.

3. Release the mouse button.

   Windows starts the application associated with the document, places the document in the print queue, closes the application, and background prints the spooled files.

TIP You can select multiple documents to print and then drag them to the desktop printer icon. The documents can be associated with different applications. Windows will start and close each application.

(See also "Copying and Moving: Drag and Drop" in the "Applications and Accessories" part of this book.)

Installing: Adding a New Printer

Windows 95 uses the Add Printer Wizard to assist you in installing a printer. If your printer is not already installed, run the Wizard to add the printer.

Steps

1. Double-click My Computer and then double-click the Printers folder icon. Double-click the Add Printer icon to start the Add Printer Wizard. Choose Next. Select the Local Printer option button (to install a printer directly attached to your printer) and then click Next again.

2. Select the printer's manufacturer in the Manufacturers list box. Select the specific printer in the Printers list box and then choose Next.

   If your printer is not on the list, either choose the Generic Manufacturer and Generic/Text Only printer or click the Have Disk button and follow the instructions to install a vendor-supplied driver.

3. Choose the printer port, typically LPT1, and then click the Configure Port button. Check the Spool MS-DOS Print Jobs and the Check Port State Before Printing check boxes. Choose OK and then choose Next.

4. In the Printer Name text box, type a name for the printer or keep the name that is displayed. Select the Yes option button if you want Windows-based programs to use this printer as the default printer. (If a different printer is the default printer, choose No.) Choose Next.

5. Select Yes if you want to print a test page, and then choose Finish. The test page prints (if you selected Yes). The Wizard copies the printer drivers to your system, prompting for the Windows 95 disks or CD if needed.

TIP Another way to open the Printers folder is by choosing Start, Settings, Printers.

Installing: Deleting an Existing Printer

If you no longer need a printer that is installed in Windows 95, you can delete it from the Printers folder window.

Steps

1. Double-click My Computer and then double-click the Printers folder icon.

2. Select the printer you want to delete. Choose File, Delete. Windows asks if you are sure that you want to delete the printer.

3. Choose Yes. The printer icon is deleted.

   Windows asks if it can remove files that were used only for this printer. Choose Yes. If you plan to reattach this printer in the future, choose No.

 TIP   If a printer has a desktop icon, you can right-click the icon and then choose Delete from the shortcut menu to delete the printer.

Installing: Renaming an Existing Printer

The Add Printer Wizard gives you an option to name the printer when you install it. You can rename the printer later without reinstalling it. The name is changed throughout Windows after you rename the printer.

Steps

1. Double-click My Computer and then double-click the Printers folder icon.

2. Select the printer you want to rename. Choose File, Rename.

3. Type a new name to replace the highlighted name. Press Enter.

TIP   If a printer has a desktop icon, you can right-click the icon and then choose Rename from the shortcut menu to rename the printer.

Print Jobs: Canceling

Use the Print Manager to control *print jobs*. You can cancel a print job in the *print queue* even if it has started to print.

Steps

1. Open the Print Manager by double-clicking the printer's icon in the Printers folder.
2. Select one or more documents from the print queue list.
3. Choose Document, Cancel Printing.

TIP   To cancel printing a document quickly, right-click its entry in the print queue and then choose Cancel Printing in the shortcut menu.

> **CAUTION**   When you cancel a print job, it disappears immediately from the print queue. You may want to try pausing the job first to be sure you are canceling the right job. (See also "Print Jobs: Pausing.")

Print Jobs: Checking Status

A quick way to check the status of print jobs is to point to the printer icon in the taskbar. To view more detail, you need to open the Print Manager.

Steps

1. Double-click the printer icon in the taskbar to open the Print Manager. This icon is displayed only when there are print jobs.
2. Look at the jobs in the queue and view their status in the Status column.

3. View the status bar to see the number of jobs remaining to be printed. Choose View, Status Bar to turn the status bar on and off.

Print Jobs: Pausing

You can pause a print job of a *local printer*, but not of a network printer. If the document has already started to print on a local printer, the other documents in the queue cannot print. However, you can pause the printing of a document before it starts to print and other documents will continue to print.

Steps

1. Double-click the printer icon in the taskbar to open the Print Manager.
2. Select one or more documents from the print queue list.
3. Choose Document, Pause Printing.

 TIP To pause a document quickly, right-click its entry in the print queue and then choose Pause Printing in the shortcut menu.

NOTE Pausing a print job is not the same as pausing printing. These are two different commands in Print Manager. Pause Printing, on the Printer menu, pauses all the pending print jobs, not just selected ones. Use the same command to release the printer. ▪

To print a paused document see "Print Jobs: Resuming."

Print Jobs: Purging

Purging removes all of the queued print jobs. Perhaps you realize after queuing print jobs that you chose the wrong version of a batch of documents that you want to print. You can purge all of the jobs that have not started to print.

PRINTING

Steps

1. Double-click the printer icon in the taskbar to open the Print Manager.

2. Choose Printer, Purge Print Jobs.

3. Close the Print Manager by clicking its Close button.

TROUBLESHOOTING   **The Purge Print Jobs command won't stop my print job that has started printing.** Purging the print jobs does not purge the print job currently being printed. You can reset the printer to terminate an unwanted print job.

Print Jobs: Resuming

(See "Print Jobs: Pausing" before trying to resume a print job.)

Usually you pause a print job so you can restart it later. Maybe you want to change to a different paper stock or change the toner. The job remains paused in Print Manager until you restart it or cancel it.

Steps

1. Open the Print Manager.

2. Select the paused document.

3. Choose Document, Pause Printing. The selected document no longer displays a Paused status and will begin printing in its place in the queue.

Print Manager: Opening

Print Manager is used to control *print jobs* sent to a printer. There is a separate manager for each printer. If the jobs you have sent to a printer are not so small that they go quickly to the printer's buffer, you will have time to double-click the printer icon that appears in the taskbar, near the clock. After the printer icon disappears from the taskbar, you can only control your job at the printer itself. There are other ways to open Print Manager.

Steps

1. Double-click My Computer and then double-click the Printers folder icon.

2. Double-click the printer icon for the printer you want to manage.

Printer Properties: Setting

After you install a printer in Windows, you can make changes to the configuration to customize it for different printing requirements. You make these changes in the printer's Properties sheet.

Steps

1. Choose Start, Settings, Printers and then select the printer icon for the printer you want to configure.

2. Right-click the printer icon and then choose Properties to open the Properties sheet.

   The Properties sheet contains several tabs. The Details tab is selected in Figure 3.

PRINTING

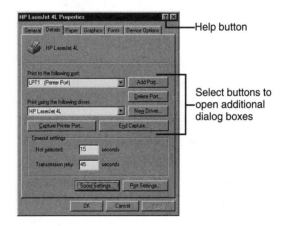

Help button

Select buttons to open additional dialog boxes

FIGURE 3
Choose each tab in the printer's Properties sheet to change the printer's settings.

3. Select each tab to view the various settings. Click the Help button (the question mark in the upper-right corner) and then click a feature to read details about that property. Properties vary according to each printer's capabilities.

4. Change settings as desired, and then choose OK to save the new settings. Choose Cancel if you prefer to abandon any changes.

TIP   You can access the printer's Properties sheet from Print Manager by choosing Printer, Properties.

(See also "Printer Properties: Using Color.")

Printer Properties: Using Color

Windows uses Kodak's Image Color Matching (ICM) technology to provide consistent color from the screen to the printed page. To benefit from this technology, choose a color printer that is compliant with Kodak's ICM specifications. Define graphics and color settings in the printer's Properties sheet.

Steps

1. Choose Start, Settings, Printers and then select the printer icon for the printer you want to configure.

2. Right-click the printer icon and then choose Properties to open the Properties sheet. Click the Graphics tab.

3. Choose from these graphics properties:

*Resolution	The number of dots per inch the printer can produce.
*Dithering	An error-correcting tool to more accurately represent an object's color and grayscale.
*Intensity	Brightness control to lighten or darken the printout, compensating for deficiencies in toner or paper quality.

*Graphics Mode   If available, controls how printing
                  information is rendered by your
                  printer.

4. Choose the Color button. If your printer does not have
   color, this button is not available. Select from the
   following color settings:

   *Color Control   Print in black and white or
                           color, with or without ICM
                           technology.

   *Color Rendering Intent Choose best setting as indi-
                           cated for presentation graph-
                           ics, photographs, or color
                           matching.

5. Choose OK twice to keep changes to settings. Notice
   there is a Restore Defaults button on each page of the
   Properties sheet to return to the defaults for the selected
   printer.

Printing: From MS-DOS Applications

Windows 95 supports printing from MS-DOS applications,
even in the same print stream with *print jobs* from Windows
applications. You can use the Print Manager to queue your
MS-DOS print jobs.

Steps
1. Open the Print Manager.
2. In the MS-DOS application, choose the print command,
   often File, Print.

A short print job may seem to go directly to the local printer,
but it is actually spooled by Windows (unless that property is
disabled in the printer's properties). If you print a larger file,
you should see the job appear in Print Manager. There you can
pause or cancel the job as needed.

(See also "Print Jobs: Pausing" and "Print Jobs: Canceling.")

Printing: From Windows Applications

Printing a document is similar in most Windows applications. You can choose File, Print to select options in a Print dialog box. The dialog box allows you to change the page range to print, number of copies, collating, default tray, resolution, and many more options that vary with the specific printer.

CAUTION A Print button on the application's toolbar may print the entire document without prompting for any options. Until you know the action of the Print button, don't choose it unless you want to print the entire document to the default printer. Use the File, Print command to open the Print dialog box.

Steps

1. Open a document to print and then choose the application's print command, usually File, Print.

2. Select the desired printer from the Name drop-down list. Select the number of copies you want to print in the Number of Copies spin box.

3. Specify the print range. The default is All. Alternatively, you can usually enter a range of pages. If you have selected text, you can usually choose the Selection option to print only the selected text.

4. Choose from the other available options. The application's documentation may be helpful in explaining its more complex printing options.

5. Make sure the printer is ready, and then choose OK.

The Print dialog box closes during printing. You may see a printing status window appear. Or you may notice the Print Manager icon in the taskbar. (See also "Print Manager: Opening.")

TROUBLESHOOTING **I chose OK in the Print dialog box, but nothing printed.** Make sure the printer is plugged in and turned on. Check Print Manager's Printer menu to see that the printer is the system default. Verify that the printer is connected to the correct port and is set up in Device Manager.

PRINTING

Equipment Configuration

Windows 95 is designed with a set of tools to assist you with the tasks of installing hardware drivers, and locating and resolving resource conflicts. This part of the book looks at installing and configuring the necessary files, modems, CD-ROM drives, and other devices, as well as locating and resolving problems between Windows 95 and the computer resources.

CD-ROM Drive: Changing Playback and Recording Settings

To set the Playback and Recording Volume controls, repeat the steps in the previous task, "CD-ROM Drive: Changing Volume Settings." First select Playback in the Properties dialog box and make the adjustments, then select Recording and make the recording adjustments.

Steps

1. Click Start (or press Alt+S) and select Programs, Accessories, Multimedia, Volume Control to open the Volume Control dialog box. Or, right-click the Volume Control icon (a speaker) on the taskbar and select Volume Control.

2. Select Options, Properties to open the Properties dialog box. Click the Playback option button in the Properties dialog box and check the check boxes to the left of the Volume Control, Line-In, Wave, and MIDI options in the Show the Following Volume Controls list box to adjust the checked devices.

3. Click the Recording option button and check the check boxes next to the Line-In and Microphone options to adjust the selected devices.

4. Click OK to return to the Volume Control and adjust the Balance and Volume Control settings.

CD-ROM Drive: Changing Volume Settings

The Volume Control tool, found on the Accessories menu on the Multimedia menu and on the taskbar, is used to adjust the volume and balance of sound being recorded and played back. You select from the Playback, Recording, or Other (input) options in the Properties dialog box. Select Options, Properties, and then make the desired adjustments in the Volume Control dialog box.

NOTE If Volume Control is not in the Accessories menu, see "Windows Components: Adding and Removing" in the "Customizing Windows 95" part of this book.

Steps

1. Click Start (or press Alt+S) and select Programs, Accessories, Multimedia, Volume Control to open the Volume Control dialog box. Or, right-click the Volume Control icon (a speaker) on the taskbar and select Volume Control.

2. Select Options, Properties to open the Properties dialog box. Select either the Playback, Recording, or Other option button in the Adjust Volume For group to determine what type of devices you want to change. Then, place a check mark in the check box next to the desired device(s) in the Show the Following Volume Controls group immediately below. Click OK to return to the Volume Control dialog box.

3. Click the vertical bar in the appropriate volume control to raise or lower the volume of the desired device.

4. Click to the left or right of the Balance pointer to adjust the balance between your two channels.

5. Select Options, Exit to close the Volume Control dialog box and return to the desktop.

NOTE To turn off the sound for all devices, place a check mark in the Mute All check box under Volume Control. To mute only specific displayed devices, place a check mark in the Mute check box of the specific device control. ■

CD-ROM Drive: Configuring Auto Insertion Notification

Windows 95 is configurable for automatically running CD-ROMs with AutoRun capability, such as the Office 97 Setup CD. Select the Auto Insertion Notification option in the CD-ROM Drive Properties dialog box opened from the Device Manager.

Steps

1. Click Start (or press Alt+S) and select Settings, Control Panel to open the Control Panel folder. Double-click the System icon to open the System Properties dialog box. Click the Device Manager tab to bring the Device Manager property sheet to the front.

2. Open the CD-ROM class by clicking the + to the left of the class name. Highlight a CD-ROM drive in the list below the class name and click the Properties button. Click the Settings tab in the Properties dialog box to bring the Settings property sheet to the front.

3. Click the Auto Insert Notification check box at the bottom of the Options group in the middle of the dialog box.

4. When you have made the desired changes, click the OK buttons in each of the dialog boxes to close the boxes, apply the changes, and return to the desktop. Click the Cancel button in any of the dialog boxes to cancel the changes and close the dialog box.

EQUIPMENT CONFIGURATION

When the Auto Insert notification option is enabled, inserting AutoRun-capable CDs will replace the CD's icon in the My Computer window and in the Windows Explorer. This will autostart the program or music on the CD.

CD-ROM Drive: Installing a Writable CD-ROM Drive

A writable CD-ROM drive (CD-R) is an affordable option for use in the home and small office settings. A CD-R drive can write to CD media once or in multi-sessions, writing to unused sections of the CD until it is full. Many CD media manufacturers guarantee the media for 100 years.

NOTE CD-ROM drives are installed in PCs using either an Enhanced IDE controller or a SCSI (Small Computer System Interface) controller. A standard IDE (Integrated Drive Electronics) controller in PCs as recent as 1996 is not designed to handle CD-ROM drives. An upgrade to an Enhanced IDE (EIDE) controller is necessary when adding an IDE CD-ROM drive to an older PC. ▦

Steps

1. Turn off the power to your computer and disconnect all cables. Open the computer case and place the case so that you can easily access the drive bay and controller card. Insert the CD-ROM drive in an empty drive bay and secure it with screws.

2. Attach the interface cable between the CD-ROM drive and the interface, located on an expansion card or on the motherboard depending on your computer. Plug the power cable between the drive and the computer power supply. Connect all additional cables between the drive and your sound card. (If you are installing a sound card at the same time, install the sound card first.)

3. If Windows 95 does not automatically sense the drive and install the necessary software drivers, run the Add

New Hardware Wizard. ClickStart (or press Alt+S) and select Settings, Control Panel, to open the Control Panel folder. Double-click the Add New Hardware icon to open the Add New Hardware Wizard.

4. Follow the steps in the Wizard to automatically install the software drivers. The second window of the Wizard asks you, Do you want Windows to search for your new hardware? Leave the Yes (Recommended) option selected to let Windows find the new drive.

5. When you have installed the CD-ROM drive, put one of your CDs in the drive, placing it in a CD caddy first if required. Double-click the My Computer icon to display the drives. Then, double-click the CD-ROM drive icon to open the CD and display the files on the CD.

Device Manager: Checking for Resource Conflicts

The Device Manager property sheet in the System program, found in the Control Panel, is used to review hardware settings and to determine where devices may have conflicts. When you open the System program and click the Device Manager tab, opening the property sheet, problems are displayed in the Class/Device list with an exclamation point.

NOTE   A red X displayed on the device icon in the Devices list box is used to indicate that the hardware device has been assigned to a Hardware Profile configuration that was not loaded for the current Windows 95 session. ▓

Steps

1. Click Start (or press Alt+S) and select Settings, Control Panel to open the Control Panel folder. Double-click the System icon to open the System Properties dialog box. Click the Device Manager tab to bring the Device Manager property sheet to the front.

EQUIPMENT CONFIGURATION

2. If there is a resource conflict, the Class group will be opened (indicated with a - to the left of the Class group name instead of a +). Scroll down the list until you see the exclamation point icon in front of the name of the device with a conflict or other problem.

3. Highlight the name of the device and click the Properties button on the button row directly below the list box. The Properties dialog box for the device is opened.

4. A Windows 95 message is displayed in the Device Status box in the center of the General property sheet indicating the basic problem and the steps Windows recommends to solve the problem. The message may also display a problem code and number that can be useful when troubleshooting or consulting with a tech support service.

   If the problem persists, refer to the manual provided with the offending hardware for possible solutions.

5. When you have made the desired changes, click the OK buttons in each of the dialog boxes to close the boxes, apply the changes, and return to the desktop. Click the Cancel button in any of the dialog boxes to cancel the changes and close the box.

NOTE If there is a red X icon in front of a device name in the Devices list box, highlight the device and click the Properties button, opening the Properties dialog box. Click the check box to the left of the configuration used to start Windows 95 in the Device Usage box at the bottom of the General properties sheet. The device will then be activated for use with Windows. ▪

NOTE Version B of Windows 95 does not contain a Device Usage box in the Device Usage dialog box. It contains two check boxes, called Disable in This Hardware Profile and Remove from This Hardware Profile. Choose the appropriate option. ▪

Device Manager: Examining Your Computer Hardware

The Device Manager in the System program, located in the Control Panel, can provide you with a summary or complete system resource printout. A summary report is provided regardless of whether you have selected the View Devices by Type option button or View Devices by Connection option button in the Device Manager.

The System Summary report provides the following information:

- System Summary
- IRQ (Interrupt ReQuest) Summary
- I/O (Input/Output) Port Summary
- Upper Memory Usage Summary
- DMA (Direct Memory Access) Usage Summary

The All Devices and System Summary report provides the following information in addition to the System Summary report:

- Memory Summary
- Disk Drive information
- System Device information

The additional information in the All Devices report includes Class, Device, Resources (if any are in use), and Device Drivers. If Resources are in use, the appropriate IRQ, I/O, and MEM information is listed immediately below the device name in the report.

The Selected Class or Device report provides the following information, if appropriate:

- Class
- Device
- Resources

EQUIPMENT CONFIGURATION

- IRQ
- I/O
- MEM

Steps

1. Click Start (or press Alt+S) and select Settings, Control Panel to open the Control Panel folder. Double-click the System icon to open the System Properties dialog box. Click the Device Manager tab to bring the Device Manager property sheet to the front.

2. Click the View Devices by Type option button to list all devices by class. To print a report for a specific class or device, highlight the name in the Devices list box. Click the Print button to open the Print dialog box.

3. Select from the System Summary, Selected Class or Device (available only if a class or device is highlighted in the Device Manager), or the All Devices and System Summary option button to specify the type of report to print.

4. Click OK in the Print dialog box to print the report on the selected output device. You are returned to the Device Manager after the printout is finished.

5. When you have made any desired changes, click the OK buttons in each of the dialog boxes to close the boxes, apply the changes, and return to the desktop. Click the Cancel button in any of the dialog boxes to cancel the changes and close the box.

You can use the All Devices and System Summary report to determine if you may have a potential conflict with new hardware that you are preparing to install in the computer. Print the report and highlight all IRQ, I/O, and MEM settings and then compare these to the settings that the new device(s) can be set to.

NOTE While Windows 95 will attempt to set up the new and existing hardware to avoid any conflicts, it is a good practice to know what the settings are before installing new equipment. ■

Hardware: Adding New

Windows 95 provides a tool, the Add New Hardware Wizard, to aid in the configuration of Windows' drivers for new equipment. The Wizard detects installed hardware, both Plug and Play and *legacy* (older, non-Plug and Play) devices, checks the results against the list of previously installed hardware, and installs drivers for the newfound devices.

NOTE   If your new hardware is not quite Plug and Play, when Windows 95 finds that device, but cannot identify the specific model, you can finish the configuration in the Device Manager (part of the System program, also found in the Control Panel). (See also "Device Manager: Checking for Resource Conflicts.")

Steps

1. Click Start (or press Alt+S) and select Settings, Control Panel to open the Control Panel folder. Double-click the Add New Hardware icon to open the Add New Hardware Wizard. Click the Next button in the first screen for the Wizard.

2. Leave the Yes (Recommended) option selected in answer to the Do You Want Windows to Search for Your New Hardware? question in the second screen. Click the Next button to move to the next screen.

3. The third screen in the Wizard tells you that the Wizard is now going to look for new hardware. Click the Next button to open the fourth screen and start the search. A thermometer gauge shows the progress the Add New Hardware Wizard is making in checking the hardware and comparing the results against the existing configuration.

4. When all new hardware has been identified, the Wizard advances you to a fifth screen. Click the Details button to open the Detected list box. Click the Finish button to allow the Wizard to load the required driver files.

EQUIPMENT CONFIGURATION

5. If the Add New Hardware Wizard cannot locate the required files on your hard drive, you are prompted to place the CD-ROM or floppy disk(s) in the appropriate drive. When the necessary files have been loaded, click the Restart button to restart Windows 95, loading the new drivers.

The Add New Hardware Wizard is used primarily to configure device controllers, such as video cards. To add a monitor, double-click the Display icon in the Control Panel and click the Change Display Adapter button to select from the lists of monitors and video display cards.

NOTE   If you select the No option in answer to the Do You Want Windows to Search for Your New Hardware? question in the second screen of the Wizard, highlight the type of hardware device you are installing from the Hardware Types list box and click the Next button to open the Manufacturers and Models screen. Highlight the manufacturer's name in the Manufacturers list box and then select the specific device from the Models list. Click the Have Disk button to use drivers provided by the manufacturer instead of the drivers included with Windows 95. (If a device was made after Windows was published, the manufacturer may provide better drivers than the default drivers picked by the Wizard.) ▩

Hardware: Determining If Your Computer Supports Plug and Play

A Plug and Play-compatible motherboard provides your computer with the best resource to run Windows 95. Windows 95 can determine whether your system motherboard is Plug and Play-compatible, displaying the results in the Device Manager window of the System program under System Devices.

Steps

1. Click Start (or press Alt+S) and select Settings, Control Panel to open the Control Panel folder. Double-click the System icon to open the System Properties dialog box.

Click the Device Manager tab to bring the Device Manager property sheet to the front.

2. Click the + next to System Devices in the Class/Device list to open the list. If your system has a Plug and Play-compatible motherboard, a driver, such as ISA Plug and Play bus with VL slots, will be included in the System Devices list.

3. If an exclamation point is displayed on the icon, there is a problem and the driver is not loaded. Highlight the device name and click the Properties button to review the description of the problem.

4. When you have made the desired changes, click the OK buttons in each of the dialog boxes to close the boxes, apply the changes, and return to the desktop. Click the Cancel button in any of the dialog boxes to cancel the changes and close the box.

Hardware Profiles: Copying and Naming

You can create additional hardware profiles, each with a different configuration, for the changing equipment you use. The first step is to create a new profile in addition to the original profile created by Windows 95. The original profile is installed by Windows with the name Original Configuration on most computers. Some custom installations performed at the factory by laptop manufacturers may name the original profile as Undocked, to reflect the normal mode the laptop will be used in.

When a profile is highlighted and copied, its exact configuration is assumed by the new copy. Change the name to reflect the type of configuration or usage the profile is used in, such as Undocked and Docked for a laptop. The name of a profile can be changed at any time and all hardware setups will be updated with the new name.

Steps

1. Click Start (or press Alt+S) and select Settings, Control Panel to open the Control Panel folder. Double-click the System icon to open the System Properties dialog box.

EQUIPMENT CONFIGURATION

Click the Hardware Profiles tab to bring the Hardware
Profiles property sheet to the front.

2. Highlight the hardware profile in the list box and click
   Copy.

3. Type a new name for the profile over the highlighted
   original name in the To field in the Copy Profile dialog
   box and click OK.

4. Click Rename to change the name of the highlighted
   profile. Change the name in the To field in the Rename
   Profile dialog box and click OK.

5. When you have made the desired changes, click the OK
   button to close the boxes, apply the changes, and return
   to the desktop. Click the Cancel button in any of the
   dialog boxes to cancel the changes and close the box.

(See also "Hardware Profiles: Customizing" to define which
equipment is used in which profile.)

Hardware Profiles: Creating

You can create additional hardware profiles, each with a different configuration, for the various equipment you use. A laptop
used with and without a docking bay is a prime system for
creating additional profiles, the original for the Undocked
configuration and the copy named for the Docked setup.

Steps

1. A docking station can be configured with additional
   equipment that you can select when you start Windows
   95, loading exactly the drivers that you need and getting
   the most out of your different equipment.

2. When you restart Windows 95, you are prompted to
   select the profile to include as Windows is loaded. When
   you restart, you can check the settings through the
   Device Manager.

(See also "Hardware Profiles: Copying and Naming" and
"Hardware Profiles: Customizing.")

Hardware Profiles: Customizing

When you have different equipment that you use with your computer under different circumstances, you can create additional hardware profiles. After copying and naming a new profile in the Hardware Profiles property sheet, the configuration is customized in the Device Manager property sheet.

NOTE Check with your system administrator before making changes to any hardware profiles files concerning network connections. ■

Steps

1. Click Start (or press Alt+S) and select Settings, Control Panel to open the Control Panel folder. Double-click the System icon to open the System Properties dialog box. Click the Device Manager tab to bring the Device Manager property sheet to the front.

2. Open a class by clicking the + to the left of the class name. Highlight a device in the list below the class name and click the Properties button. Click the General tab in the Properties dialog box to bring the General property sheet to the front if it is not already visible.

3. Click the check box to the left of the hardware profile names displayed in the Device Usage box at the bottom to place or remove a check mark in the check box. When a check box is checked, the selected device being customized will be set up if the profile is used at startup. Click OK after checking all profiles that you want the device to be in.

4. Customize any other devices that are used specifically in one profile or another.

5. When you have made the desired changes, click the OK buttons in each of the dialog boxes to close the boxes, apply the changes, and return to the desktop. Click the Cancel button in any of the dialog boxes to cancel the changes and close the box.

EQUIPMENT CONFIGURATION

> **NOTE** Devices that are not loaded by the hardware profile
> used for startup are shown in the Device Manager with a red X
> mark on the device icon. When you highlight the device, open
> the Properties dialog box, and check the currently loaded pro-
> file check box. The appropriate drivers are loaded and the X
> is removed from the icon as soon as you return to the Device
> Manager. ■

Keyboard: Configuring

The Keyboard Properties control program in the Control Panel
is used to customize the way you use your keyboard. You set
your keyboard for the way that you type, how fast the keyboard places repeat characters, and what language you are
working in.

> **NOTE** When more than one language is set up in Windows 95,
> the first one installed is used as the default. The default language
> can be changed in the Keyboard Properties program. Use the
> Language properties sheet in the Keyboard Properties program to
> select the new language from the 49 different languages and
> language versions in the Language drop-down list box. Reboot
> the computer to load the new language keyboard drivers. ■

Steps

1. Click Start (or press Alt+S) and select Settings, Control
   Panel to open the Control Panel folder. Double-click
   the Keyboard icon to open the Keyboard Properties
   dialog box.

2. Click the General tab to bring the General property
   sheet to the front. Click the Change button to the right of
   the Keyboard Type field to open the Select Device dialog
   box and select a different keyboard setup.

3. Click the Show All Devices option button in the bottom-
   left corner of the dialog box to see a list of all keyboards.
   If you have a disk with drivers from the keyboard

manufacturer, click the Have Disk button to open the Install From Disk dialog box, put the disk in a floppy drive, select the appropriate drive in the Copy Manufacturer's Files From drop-down list box, and follow the instructions to copy the file(s) to your system.

4. Click the Language tab to bring the Language property sheet to the front, then click the Speed tab to bring the Speed property sheet to the front.

5. When you have made the desired changes, click the OK buttons in each of the dialog boxes to close the boxes, apply the changes, and return to the desktop. Click the Cancel button in any of the dialog boxes to cancel the changes and close the box.

Modem: Configuring

Windows 95 installs the drivers for your modem using the best settings it has in the drivers. When you need to make changes, possibly because an online service provider or Bulletin Board Service (BBS) that you want to connect to requires different settings, use the Modem Properties program in the Control Panel to make the necessary changes.

NOTE The modem settings included in the modem drivers are standard for accessing common online services, such as CompuServe, America Online, and Internet ISPs (Internet Service Providers). █

Steps

1. Click Start (or press Alt+S) and select Settings, Control Panel to open the Control Panel folder. Double-click the Modems icon to open the Modems Properties dialog box. Highlight the modem to be configured if you have set up more than one. Click the Properties button to bring the Properties property sheet to the front for the highlighted modem.

2. Click the General tab to bring the General property sheet to the front, and click the Port drop-down list box

EQUIPMENT CONFIGURATION

to select from the available communications ports. Click the horizontal bar of the Speaker Volume control to adjust the loudness of the modem speaker. To change the maximum connect speed of the modem, click the Maximum Speed drop-down list box and select from the speed options.

3. Click the Connection tab to bring the Connection property sheet to the front. Set the Data Bits, Parity, and Stop Bits values in the drop-down list boxes in the Connection Preferences group at the top of the Connection property sheet. Place check marks in the Wait for Dial Tone Before Dialing, Cancel the Call If Not Connected Within Secs, and Disconnect a Call If Idle For More Than Mins to customize your connection.

4. Click the Port Settings button to open the Advanced Port Settings dialog box and modify the Use FIFO Buffers (First-In-First-Out), Receive Buffer, and Transmit Buffer settings. The settings can be returned to the Windows default by clicking the Defaults button. Return to the Modems Properties dialog box by clicking OK or Cancel.

5. Click the Advanced button to open the Advanced Connection Settings dialog box. Check the Use Error Control check box to enable modem error correcting software and check Required to Connect, Compress Data, or Use Cellular Protocol to control the error correcting features. Check the Use Flow Control check box and select either the Hardware (RTS/CTS) or Software (XON/XOFF) option button to enable flow control and indicate the type of control. Return to the Modems Properties dialog box by clicking OK or Cancel.

6. When you have made the desired changes, click the OK buttons in each of the dialog boxes to close the boxes, apply the changes, and return to the desktop. Click the Cancel button in any of the dialog boxes to cancel the changes and close the box.

Modem: Installing Legacy

You may have purchased a modem, or had one given to you, that was manufactured before standards for Plug and Play were defined. When you install the modem in Windows 95, the Install New Modem Wizard will install a generic driver that it determines will work with the modem found. You can specify the modem manually in the Wizard and pick a better driver, or use the driver files provided by the manufacturer on a disk or downloaded from online.

Steps

1. Click Start (or press Alt+S) and select Settings, Control Panel to open the Control Panel folder. Double-click the Modem icon to open the Modem dialog box. Click the Add button to open the Install New Modem Wizard.

2. Click the Don't Detect My Modem; I Will Select It From a List check box to go straight to the Manufacturers list when you click Next. If you want to select a driver set other than the modem driver set indicated, click the Change button. The Manufacturers and Models lists are opened.

3. Pick the manufacturer from the Manufacturers list and then highlight the modem in the Models list. If you intend to use a driver provided by the manufacturer on a disk or downloaded from online, click the Have Disk button and follow the steps in the Install From Disk dialog box.

4. After picking your manufacturer and model or finishing the installation from a disk, click the Next button. In the next screen, select the communications port from the list and click Next.

5. When the Install New Modem Wizard has finished installing the drivers, click Finish to return to the desktop.

You delete modem drivers in the Modem Properties dialog box by highlighting the modem name and clicking the Remove button.

EQUIPMENT CONFIGURATION

Modem: Installing Plug and Play

Plug and Play modems are the simplest type of modem to configure. Simply put the modem in the computer and start Windows 95. There are two types of true Plug and Play modems—internal modems installed in an ISA (Industry Standard Architecture) slot, and PC Cards (PCMCIA) used predominantly in laptops.

Internal Plug and Play modems require that you open the computer, install the modem in an expansion slot, and restart the computer. PC Card modems can be installed in laptops with the computer on or off.

Steps

1. Locate a PC Card slot on your computer and slide the modem into the slot. Turn on your computer if it is off.

2. Windows 95 detects the new modem when it starts and automatically loads the modem drivers.

3. Click Start (or press Alt+S) and select Settings, Control Panel to open the Control Panel folder. Double-click the Modem icon to open the Modem dialog box. The modem is displayed in the Modem Properties dialog box.

4. Click the Properties button to check the modem settings.

5. When you have made the desired changes, click the OK buttons in each of the dialog boxes to close the boxes, apply the changes, and return to the desktop. Click the Cancel button in any of the dialog boxes to cancel the changes and close the box.

Installing an internal modem is just as simple, except that you need to have the computer off and there needs to be an available slot to put the modem in.

Modem: Setting to Dial

You need to configure the Windows 95 dialing properties to make connecting to all types of services easier by providing

home/office information and handling call waiting and calling
card requirements.

Steps

1. Click Start (or press Alt+S) and select Settings, Control
   Panel to open the Control Panel folder. Double-click the
   Modems icon to open the Modems Properties dialog
   box. Highlight the modem to be configured if you have
   set up more than one. Click the Properties button to
   bring the Properties property sheet to the front for the
   highlighted modem.

2. Click the General tab to bring the General property
   sheet to the front. Click the Dialing Properties button to
   open the Dialing Properties dialog box. Enter your area
   code in the The Area Code Is field and select the country
   or region you are setting up in the I Am In field to define
   the default location.

3. In the To Access An Outside Line, First Dial For Local
   field, enter a number needed to get an outside phone line
   if your telephone system requires it. If you use a calling
   card, click the Dial Using Calling Card check box and
   select the calling card provider in the Change Calling
   Card dialog box.

4. Leave the check mark in the check box labeled This
   Location Has Call Waiting if you have a call waiting
   feature on the telephone line you intend to use. To
   disable call waiting, select either *70, 70#, 1170, or the
   blank field in the To Disable It, Dial drop-down list box.
   If your telephone company does not use one of the three
   predefined codes, enter the specific code in the blank
   field.

5. When you have made the desired changes, click the OK
   buttons in each of the dialog boxes to close the boxes,
   apply the changes, and return to the desktop. Click the
   Cancel button in any of the dialog boxes to cancel the
   changes and close the box.

EQUIPMENT CONFIGURATION

The information you enter in the Dialing Properties dialog box is used by Windows 95 telecommunications programs, such as Microsoft Fax, Phone Dialer, and Dial-Up Networking.

Modem: Using Drivers Provided by Manufacturers

Windows 95 is shipped with a wealth of drivers for a great variety of modems. But as time passes, new modems are manufactured that are not included in the Windows drivers database, and new drivers are developed by the manufacturers. Install the drivers for your modem through the Install New Modem Wizard opened from the Modem Properties dialog box.

Steps

1. Click Start (or press Alt+S) and select Settings, Control Panel to open the Control Panel folder. Double-click the Modem icon to open the Modem dialog box. Click the Add button to open the Install New Modem Wizard.

2. Click the Don't Detect My Modem; I Will Select It From a List check box and click the Next button. If your new modem is not in the Manufacturers and Models list boxes and you have the drivers from the manufacturer, click the Have Disk button.

3. Insert the disk that has the .INF file in drive A: (or B:) and click OK. If you have downloaded new drivers from an online service to your computer, instead of inserting a floppy disk, click the Browse button to select the folder that the drivers were downloaded into. Click the OK buttons to return to the Install New Modem Wizard and click Next.

4. Select the communications port the modem is set for or connected to (if it is external) and click Next.

5. Click the Finish button in the last screen of the Wizard to return to the desktop.

Modem: Using the Diagnostic Tool

Windows 95 provides a tool for diagnosing problems with your modem. The Diagnostics tool identifies the port that each modem is installed on, the Interrupt address, I/O Address, type of serial UART chip (Universal Asynchronous Receiver/ Transmitter), and the highest possible connection speed for the inspected components.

Steps

1. Click Start (or press Alt+S) and select Settings, Control Panel to open the Control Panel folder. Double-click the Modem icon to open the Modem dialog box. Click the Diagnostics tab to bring the Modem Diagnostics tool to the front.

2. Highlight the communications port that the modem is attached to in the Port list. Click the More Info button to open the More Info information box.

3. Review the information in the Port Information group at the top and in the Modem Response Code group at the bottom of the dialog box. Click OK to return to the Modem Properties dialog box.

4. Click the Driver button to view the communications driver currently used by Windows 95.

5. When you have reviewed the information in either information box, click the OK buttons in each dialog box to close the boxes and return to the desktop. Click the Cancel button in any of the dialog boxes to cancel the changes and close the box.

The serial UART chip, identified in the More Info information box, may limit the speed at which your modem can communicate. A 16550 UART chip is required to get speeds above 14,400 bps (bits per second).

NOTE The information displayed in the Modem Return Code group at the bottom of the More Info information box is made up of the codes passed to the modem to configure it to communicate with other modems. The information returned in the window is specific to the modem, not Windows 95 A or B. An important

EQUIPMENT CONFIGURATION

piece of information to check is the EPROM Date. This is the date on which the chip that holds the program code for the modem was created. The date is specific to the modem model and manufacturer and is used in diagnostic and upgrade situations. Many currently available modems can be updated by users from programs downloaded from the manufacturer's BBS or possibly Internet Web site. ■

Mouse: Changing Button Settings

Use the Mouse Properties program to customize your mouse for left-handed use and to adjust the mouse driver to recognize how you double-click with the mouse.

Steps

1. Click Start (or press Alt+S) and select Settings, Control Panel to open the Control Panel folder. Double-click the Mouse icon to open the Mouse Properties dialog box.

2. Click the Buttons tab to bring the Buttons property sheet to the front. Click either the Right-handed or the Left-handed option button, changing the functions performed when you click the left and right mouse buttons.

3. If Windows does not seem to always respond when you double-click, adjust the Double-click Speed indicator at the bottom of the Buttons property sheet and test the new setting in the Test Area of the property sheet.

4. Click the Apply button to apply changes, leaving the dialog box open.

5. When you have made the desired changes, click the OK buttons in each of the dialog boxes to close the boxes, apply the changes, and return to the desktop. Click the Cancel button in any of the dialog boxes to cancel the changes and close the box.

Mouse: Configuring Mouse Motion

Windows 95 can be customized for the way that the mouse appears to you on the screen. Using the Motion property sheet in the Mouse Properties program, you can set the pointer speed and pointer trail.

Steps

1. Click Start (or press Alt+S) and select Settings, Control Panel to open the Control Panel folder. Double-click the Mouse icon to open the Mouse Properties dialog box.

2. Click the Motion tab to bring the Motion property sheet to the front. Click and drag the speed indicator in the Pointer Speed field to speed up or slow down how fast the mouse pointer follows mouse movement. Click the Apply button in the bottom-right corner of the dialog box to apply the change and to experience how the change affects the mouse pointer movement.

3. Click the Show Pointer Trails check box in the Pointer Trail group to display pointer trails (an echo of the pointer) as the mouse moves. Click and drag the indicator in the field below to control the appearance of the mouse pointer trail as it follows mouse movement. Click the Apply button in the bottom-right corner of the dialog box to apply the change.

4. Click the Show Pointer Trails check box again, removing the check mark, to turn the pointer trails feature off.

5. When you have made the desired changes, click the OK button to close the dialog box, apply the changes, and return to the desktop. Click the Cancel button in the dialog box to cancel the changes and close the box.

NOTE Turning pointer trails on is helpful when you are using a laptop. Many times, the mouse cursor is lost on the LCD screen, and the pointer trail allows you to track the movement of the mouse in less than optimal lighting conditions where LCD screens have problems. ▪

Mouse: Installing a Different Mouse

You may find that you need to change your mouse permanently or use several different pointing devices during the

EQUIPMENT CONFIGURATION

course of your work. You add additional mouse or pointing device drivers in the General property sheet of the Mouse Properties program.

NOTE A laptop user may want to configure Windows 95 for both the internal pointing device, whether it is a trackball, trackpad, or some other device, and an external mouse. ▉

Steps

1. Click Start (or press Alt+S) and select Settings, Control Panel to open the Control Panel folder. Double-click the Mouse icon to open the Mouse Properties dialog box.

2. Click the General tab to bring the General property sheet to the front. The currently installed mouse driver is displayed in the Name field. Click the Change button to the right to open the Select Device dialog box.

3. Click the Show All Devices option button in the bottom-left corner to view all Windows 95-provided manufacturers and models. Highlight the manufacturer's name in the Manufacturers list box and then select the specific mouse device in the Models list box. Click OK to return to the Mouse Properties dialog box.

4. Click the Apply button in the bottom-right corner of the dialog box to apply the new driver. If the mouse does not seem to be operating properly, repeat Steps 2-4, selecting a different driver.

5. When you have made the desired changes, click the OK buttons in each of the dialog boxes to close the boxes, apply the changes, and return to the desktop. Click the Cancel button in any of the dialog boxes to cancel the changes and close the box.

NOTE If you have a computer with two serial ports and your serial mouse is not functioning, change the serial port that the mouse is attached to and restart Windows 95. If the mouse continues to not operate, follow the previous steps to select a different mouse driver, possibly one of the Standard Mouse Types in the Manufacturers list of the Select Device dialog box.

If the serial mouse still does not work, open System (from the Control Panel) and check the Ports Class in the Device Manager to make sure that the port is configured properly. ■

Power Management: Setting Properties

Windows 95 can be configured to work with green computer systems. Green systems conserve energy by turning off different devices, such as the monitor or hard drive, when the system is turned on but not in use (usually determined by mouse or keyboard activity).

The power management settings vary between BIOS and motherboard manufacturers. The following settings are representative of a local bus motherboard with an Award BIOS chip set.

Steps

1. Click Start (or press Alt+S) and select Settings, Control Panel to open the Control Panel folder. Double-click the System icon to open the System Properties dialog box.

2. Click the Device Manager tab to bring the Device Manager sheet to the front. Click the + next to System Devices in the Class/Device list to open the list. If your system supports power management, Advanced Power Management Support will be listed under the System Devices Class.

3. Highlight Advanced Power Management Support and click the Properties button in the bottom-left corner of the Device Manager sheet. Click the Settings tab in the Advanced Power Management Support Properties dialog box to bring the Setting sheet to the front. See the Note following these steps if you are using version B of Windows 95.

4. Click the Enable Power Management Support check box to enable power management. Place a check mark in the Force APM 1.0 Mode, Disable Intel SL Support, or Disable Power Status Polling check boxes to enable those power management features.

EQUIPMENT CONFIGURATION

5. When you have made the desired changes, click the OK buttons in each of the dialog boxes to close the boxes, apply the changes, and return to the desktop. Click the Cancel button in any of the dialog boxes to cancel the changes and close the box.

NOTE These steps are based on Microsoft Windows 95, version 4.00.950 A. If your version of Windows 95 is different, your steps for this task will vary. To check your version of Windows, right-click the My Computer icon, choose Properties, and look at the System entry on the General page. ▪

NOTE To enable power management in version B of Windows 95, open the Control Panel, double-click the Power icon, and select the Power tab. In the Power Properties dialog box check the Allow Windows to Manage Power Use on This Computer check box. ▪

CAUTION If Windows 95 locks up, check whether you have enabled power management and any of the options. Remove the check mark in the Enable Power Management Support check box and restart Windows. If the problem does not occur again, the system may not be totally power management-capable.

Printers: Configuring

Windows 95 installs the printer drivers with default settings when you click the Add Printer icon in the Printers window, opened from the Start menu under Settings or from the Control Panel. The Printer Properties dialog box has different property sheets depending on its manufacturer and model, where you can specify settings. The property sheets and their options are described in the following list.

- **General** Specify a Comment, Separator Page, and Print Test Page.
- **Details** Add Port, Delete Port, Capture Printer Port, End Capture, or Print to the Following Port, Print Using

the Following Driver, New Driver, set Timeout Settings—Not Selected and Transmission Retry; Spool Settings, and Port Settings.

- **Sharing** Specify Not Shared or Shared As—Share Name, Comment, and a Password for sharing access.

- **Paper** Pick a Paper Size, Layout—1 up, 2 up, 4 up (if PostScript-capable printer); Orientation—Portrait or Landscape, Paper Source, number of Copies, and define the Unprintable Area.

- **Graphics** Select the Resolution, Halftoning, Special— Print as a Negative Image or Print as a Mirror Image, and Scaling.

- **Fonts** Send TrueType Fonts to Printer According to the Font, Always Use Built-in Printer Fonts Instead of TrueType Fonts, or Always Use TrueType Fonts options.

- **Device Options** Available Printer Memory (in KB) and Print Quality.

- **PostScript** PostScript Output Format, PostScript Header—Download Header With Each Print Job or Assume Header is Downloaded and Retained, and Send Header Now (if your printer is PostScript-capable).

Steps

1. Click Start (or press Alt+S) and select Settings, Printers to open the Printers folder. Right-click the icon of the printer you want to configure and select Properties to open the Printer Properties dialog box.

2. Click the Details tab to bring the Details property sheet to the front. Click the New Driver button to install a new driver in the Select Device dialog box. Click OK to return to the Properties dialog box.

3. Click the Print to the Following Port drop-down list box to select a different port to connect the printer to. Click the Add Port button to add a port to the list box, including network ports if you are using a network.

EQUIPMENT CONFIGURATION

4. When you have made the desired changes, click the OK buttons in each of the dialog boxes to close the boxes, apply the changes, and return to the desktop. Click the Cancel button in any of the dialog boxes to cancel the changes and close the box.

Refer to the manual supplied with the printer to further customize the printer properties.

Sound: Configuring Audio Properties

Adjust the volume for recording and playing back sounds through the sound card in the Multimedia Properties dialog box.

Steps

1. Click Start (or press Alt+S) and select Settings, Control Panel to open the Control Panel folder. Double-click the Multimedia icon to open the Multimedia Properties dialog box.

2. Click the Audio tab to bring the Audio property sheet to the front. Click and drag the indicator in the Volume field to raise and lower the volume that audio CDs are heard through the sound system.

3. Place a check mark in the Show Volume Control on the Taskbar check box to enable control from the desktop. To open the Volume Control from the taskbar, right-click the speaker icon and select Volume Control.

4. Select CD Quality, Radio Quality, or Telephone Quality in the Preferred Quality drop-down list box. This selection affects both the quality of the recording and the amount of hard disk space used by the recording. The better the quality, the more space used to record. Click the Apply button in the bottom-right corner of the dialog box to apply the change.

5. When you have made the desired changes, click the OK buttons in each of the dialog boxes to close the boxes, apply the changes, and return to the desktop. Click the

Cancel button in any of the dialog boxes to cancel the changes and close the box.

Sound: Setting Up MIDI Output

Specify the instrument used by Windows 95 to play MIDI sound effects in the Multimedia Properties dialog box.

Steps

1. Click Start (or press Alt+S) and select Settings, Control Panel to open the Control Panel folder. Double-click the Multimedia icon to open the Multimedia Properties dialog box.

2. Click the MIDI tab to bring the MIDI property sheet to the front. Click the Single Instrument option button to select from the list of installed MIDI instruments immediately below.

3. Click the Custom Configuration option button and pick a definition from the MIDI Scheme drop-down list box. To create a new scheme or configure an existing scheme, click the Configure button to configure the instrument according to the instructions included with your MIDI devices. Click OK to return to the Multimedia Properties dialog box.

4. Click the Apply button in the bottom-right corner of the dialog box to apply the change.

5. When you have made the desired changes, click the OK buttons in each of the dialog boxes to close the boxes, apply the changes, and return to the desktop. Click the Cancel button in any of the dialog boxes to cancel the changes and close the box.

Startup Disk: Creating

A startup disk can be made at the time that you install Windows 95, or at any time to be used to restart your computer in an emergency, such as when corrupted system files are detected at normal Windows 95 startup. The startup program

EQUIPMENT CONFIGURATION

files are copied to a floppy disk, and any existing files on the disk are erased through the Add/Remove Programs utility in the Control Panel.

Steps

1. Click Start (or press Alt+S) and select Settings, Control Panel to open the Control Panel folder. Double-click the Add/Remove Programs icon to open the Add/Remove Programs Properties dialog box. Click the Startup Disk tab to bring the Startup Disk sheet to the front.

2. Click the Create Disk button to start the process. As Windows prepares to create the startup disk, it prompts you to label and insert a floppy disk in drive A:. Click the OK button. If an error occurs, a Disk Initialization Error information box will be displayed with a message describing the problem, such as Error: Disk sector was not found. Insert another disk and click OK.

3. You are returned to the Add/Remove Programs Properties dialog box (with no additional messages) when the startup disk has been successfully made. Click OK to close the dialog box and return to the desktop.

 TIP Make several startup disks because floppy disks are cheap. Open the write-protect notches to minimize the possibility of erasing or overwriting the disks.

System Properties: Changing

The properties for system-level (the motherboard) devices can be reviewed and modified through the Device Manager of the System Properties program opened from the Control Panel.

CAUTION Do not change the properties of system devices unless you have checked with your system administrator or are an advanced computer user. Changing these settings can cause your computer to lock up or not restart if set improperly. Create a startup disk, if you do not have one, before making changes to the system device properties.

Steps

1. Click Start (or press Alt+S) and select Settings, Control Panel to open the Control Panel folder. Double-click the System icon to open the System Properties dialog box. Click the Device Manager tab to bring the Device Manager sheet to the front.

2. Click the + to open the System Devices Class. Highlight the system device that you want to inspect, and click the Properties button in the bottom-left corner to open the Properties dialog box for the device.

3. The General property sheet for each system device reports the Device Type, Manufacturer, Hardware Version (if determinable by Windows 95), and Device Status. The Resources property sheet reports on any Input/Output address, Interrupt Requests, and other hardware settings. Remove the check mark in the Use Automatic Settings check box to activate the Change Settings button. Click the Change Settings button to select other device settings, confirming that there is no conflict with another device in the Conflict Information group at the bottom of the Edit Device Property dialog box.

4. Select the Settings tab (if one is available for the selected system device) to review and change device settings.

5. When you have made the desired changes, click the OK buttons in each of the dialog boxes to close the boxes, apply the changes, and return to the desktop. Click the Cancel button in any of the dialog boxes to cancel the changes and close the box.

NOTE   Some devices may not have a Resources property sheet, and some devices may have a Driver property sheet that shows the Provider, Date, and Version (of the driver); a Driver File Details button; and an Update Driver button. ▉

EQUIPMENT CONFIGURATION

System Properties: Checking Performance Settings

The performance of your system can be reviewed and modified through the System Properties program found in the Control Panel.

CAUTION   Do not change the settings in the Virtual Memory dialog box unless you have checked with your system administrator or are an advanced computer user. Changing these settings can cause your computer to lock up or not restart if set improperly. Create a startup disk, if you do not have one, before making changes to the Virtual Memory. (See also "Startup Disk: Creating.")

Steps

1. Click Start (or press Alt+S) and select Settings, Control Panel to open the Control Panel folder. Double-click the System icon to open the System Properties dialog box. Click the Performance tab to bring the Performance property sheet to the front.

2. The Performance Status group displays the current Memory, System Resources, File System, Virtual Memory, Disk Compression, and PC Cards (PCMCIA) status. To see additional information, or to change the File System, Graphics, or Virtual Memory settings, click the appropriate button in the Advanced Settings group at the bottom of the dialog box.

3. Use the File Systems Properties dialog box to optimize the settings for hard disk drives, CD-ROM drives, and to troubleshoot other file problems.

4. Adjust the use of Hardware Acceleration for graphics in the Advanced Graphics Settings dialog box, opened when you click the Graphics button in the Performance property sheet.

5. When you have made the desired changes, click the OK buttons in each of the dialog boxes to close the boxes, apply the changes, and return to the desktop. Click the Cancel button in any of the dialog boxes to cancel the changes and close the box.

(See also "System: Using Virtual Memory" in the "Disk and File Management" part of this book.)

Video: Configuring Drivers

The best device drivers that Windows 95 can determine are appropriate for your video card are installed when Windows 95 is first configured. You can configure the driver further, possibly using a different driver to get better performance from your video display card, in the System Properties program.

Steps

1. Click Start (or press Alt+S) and select Settings, Control Panel to open the Control Panel folder. Double-click the System icon to open the System Properties dialog box. Click the Device Manager tab to bring the Device Manager sheet to the front.

2. Click the + to open the Display Adapters Class. Highlight the installed video driver and click the Properties button in the bottom-left corner to open the video adapter Properties dialog box.

3. Click the Driver tab to bring the Driver property sheet to the front. The currently installed drivers are displayed in the Driver Files list box. Click the Change Driver button in the bottom-right corner of the Driver property sheet to open the Select Device dialog box.

4. Click the Show All Devices option button to see a list of all manufacturers supported directly by Windows 95. Select the manufacturer from the Manufacturers list box and then select the video card from the Models list box.

EQUIPMENT CONFIGURATION

5. When you have made the desired changes, click the OK buttons in each of the dialog boxes to close the boxes, apply the changes, and return to the desktop. Click the Cancel button in any of the dialog boxes to cancel the changes and close the box.

NOTE   If you are using version B of Windows 95, click the Driver File Details button to review the drivers in the Driver File Details dialog box. Click the Update Driver button in the bottom-right corner of the Driver property sheet to open the Update Device Driver Wizard. Windows may prompt you to insert your Windows disks or CD-ROM. ▪

Video: Configuring Video Properties

You can adjust the manner in which Windows 95 displays video clips using the Multimedia Properties dialog box opened from the Control Panel. You set the size of the video clip in a window or display it as full screen.

Steps

1. Click Start (or press Alt+S) and select Settings, Control Panel to open the Control Panel folder. Double-click the Multimedia icon to open the Multimedia Properties dialog box.

2. Click the Video tab to bring the Video property sheet to the front.

3. Click the Full Screen option button in the Show Video In group at the bottom of the sheet. As you see in the preview above the group box, the video clip will be enlarged to fill the entire screen. Click the Window option button to select either Original Size, Double Original Size, 1/16 of Screen Size, 1/4 of Screen Size, 1/2 of Screen Size, or Maximized to determine the size the video clip will be shown in a window on the desktop.

4. Click the Apply button in the bottom-right corner of the dialog box to apply the change.

5. When you have made the desired changes, click the OK buttons in each of the dialog boxes to close the boxes, apply the changes, and return to the desktop. Click the Cancel button in any of the dialog boxes to cancel the changes and close the box.

NOTE Finding the combination of screen resolution, number of colors, and fonts may require resetting these settings and rebooting several times because of the differences in video display cards and monitors. ■

Multimedia

Multimedia is considered one of the leading reasons why personal computers have been moving into the home market. Whether considering games or instructional multimedia videos, movieCDs, or Encarta from Microsoft, many people find the combination of audio and visual (video) effects irresistible.

Internet Web sites combine animation and RealAudio sound clips to entice surfers to stay and browse. By the summer of 1997, Web sites are expected to even feature 3-D visual effects, a virtual reality in your home.

Even the basic tools shipped with Windows 95, CD Player, Media Player, and Sound Recorder give a home user the ability to create multimedia events that, with a CD-R drive (a recording CD drive) and the appropriate media, can then be pressed on to a CD and shared with others.

Sound events can also be added to program events, adding an additional attention-getting device if you cannot respond to visual cues. Couple that with voice-command software shipped with many sound cards, and your computer can be used hands-free.

Audio CDs: AutoPlay

The CD Player is set up by Windows 95 to automatically start playing a music CD when the disc is inserted in the CD player.

Steps

1. Put a CD in your CD-ROM drive, using a CD caddy if required by the CD-ROM drive. The CD Player program is automatically placed on the taskbar, starting the music at the same time.

2. To disable the AutoPlay feature of the CD Player, double-click the My Computer icon on the desktop. Select View, Options to open the Options dialog box. Click the File Types tab to bring the File Types property sheet to the front. Highlight AudioCD in the Registered File Types list box and click the Edit button.

3. Highlight Play in the Actions list box and click the Edit button in the Edit File Type dialog box. The Editing Action For Type: AudioCD dialog box is opened.

4. The CD Player program is shown in the Application Used to Perform Action field with its complete path and the /play parameter following the command (separated with a space). Delete the /play parameter, click OK, and click Close in the previous dialog boxes to return to the desktop.

Audio CDs: AutoPlay on Startup

The CD Player can be set up in Windows 95 to automatically start playing a music CD when Windows is started, as long as the music CD is in the CD drive when Windows starts.

Steps

1. Before you shut down your previous Windows session, right-click the taskbar and select Properties to open the Taskbar Properties dialog box. Click the Start Menu Programs tab to bring the Start Menu Programs property sheet to the front. Click the Add button to open the Create Shortcut Wizard.

2. Type **C:\WINDOWS\CD Player.EXE /play** in the Command Line field, or click the Browse button to open the Browse dialog box. Here you can navigate to the Windows 95 folder and double-click CD Player, adding the **/play** parameter to the command in the Command Line field. Click Next to move to the Select Program Folder screen.

3. Highlight the StartUp folder and click Next. The shortcut name, CD Player, is displayed in the Select a Name

for the Shortcut field. Type a different name if you want. Click Finish to return to the Taskbar Properties dialog box and click OK to return to the desktop.

4. Leave a music CD in your CD-ROM drive when you turn off your previous Windows 95 session. If you forget and you have an external CD drive, turn the power on for the external drive and press the Eject button on the drive to open the tray and insert the CD. Close the tray by pressing the Eject button again.

5. Turn your computer system on. The CD Player program is automatically placed on the taskbar, starting the music at the same time. If a music CD is not loaded in the CD drive when Windows 95 is started, the CD Player is started and left on the taskbar. Click CD Player on the taskbar to open it on the desktop. The message, Data or no disc loaded, is displayed in the Artist field and an additional message, Please insert an audio compact disc, is displayed in the Title field.

Press the Eject button on the front of the CD drive to open the CD tray and insert a music or audio CD. Close the tray by pressing the Eject button again. If your CD drive uses a caddy, place the music CD in the caddy and insert it in the drive. Click the Play icon on the player controls toolbar to start playing.

Audio CDs: Creating a Play List

Create a play list of music to play from the CD-ROM player in your computer. A play list gives you the control to play tracks in the order that you specify, skipping tracks that you do not like. Play lists are saved by Windows 95 and are displayed when the same CD is inserted in the CD drive and the CD Player is open.

NOTE   A play list can list any track more than once, allowing you to create long-playing music sessions from one CD. ▪

MULTIMEDIA

Steps

1. Click Start (or press Alt+S) and select Programs, Accessories, Multimedia, CD Player to open the CD Player program window. If you have not placed an audio CD in the drive, the message `Please insert an audio compact disc` is displayed in the Title field of the dialog box. Put a CD in your CD-ROM drive, using a CD caddy if required by the CD-ROM drive.

2. Select Disc, Edit Play List to open the CD Player: Disc Settings dialog box. The current CD player is indicated in the Drive field; New Artist is the default title in the Artist field and New Title is the default in the Title field.

3. By default, all tracks on the CD are listed in both the Available Tracks list box and the Play List list box. To remove a single track from the play list, double-click the track name. Click the Clear All button between the two list boxes to clear all tracks from the play list.

4. Double-click a track in the Available Tracks list box to add a single track to the play list. To select several tracks, click the first track and click the last contiguous track while holding down the Shift key; then click the Add button. To add several tracks that are not listed consecutively in the Available Tracks list, single-click the track and then click each subsequent track while holding down the Ctrl key. Click OK to accept any changes.

5. Select Options, Preferences and make sure there is a check mark in the Save Settings on Exit check box to save the play list. Click OK to close the Preferences dialog box and Alt+F4 to close the CD Player.

NOTE Tracks are added to the play list in the order in which they are added. When adding multiple tracks at once, they will reflect the alphabetic order they are in when you click the Add button. ▪

Audio CDs: Editing a Play List

Play lists that you create can be customized to provide additional information such as the artist's name, album title, and the names of the songs on specific tracks. When you use the CD Player: Disc Setting dialog box, you can include information that you see on the sleeve of the jewel case (the plastic case that music CDs come in).

MULTIMEDIA

Steps

1. Click Start (or press Alt+S) and select Programs, Accessories, Multimedia, CD Player to open the CD Player program window. If you have not placed an audio CD in the drive, a message, Please insert an audio compact disc, is displayed in the Title field of the dialog box. Put a CD that you have already created a play list for in your CD-ROM drive, using a CD caddy if required.

2. Select Disc, Edit Play List to open the CD Player: Disc Settings dialog box. The current CD player is indicated in the Drive field, and New Artist is the default title in the Artist field. With the current name highlighted, simply type the name of the performer or any other related information in the Artist field. You can enter up to 49 characters in the Artist field. Press Tab to move to the Title field.

3. Replace the default title, New Title, with the title of the CD, up to 49 characters in length.

4. When a track is highlighted in the Available Tracks list box, you can give it a specific name by typing in the name in the Track field at the bottom of the dialog box and clicking the Set Name button. This gives you the ability to then see a more descriptive name (up to 39 characters) for each track when you see the track name in the Track field in the CD Player.

5. Click OK to close the dialog box and return to the CD Player. When you return to the CD Player, you see the artist name, title, and track information in the fields below the timer and player controls toolbars.

6. Select Options, Preferences and make sure there is a check mark in the Save Settings on Exit check box to save the play list. Click OK to close the Preferences dialog box and Alt+F4 to close the CD Player.

NOTE While you can enter up to 49 characters in the Artist and Title fields, and 39 in the Track field in the CD Player: Disc Settings dialog box, only the first 33 characters are displayed in each of the appropriate fields back in the CD Player. ■

Audio CDs: Playing

Playing a music or audio CD in your computer's CD player is just as easy as using a portable or other music-only player. You can attach speakers (check the output of the sound card and the requirements of the speakers first) to the sound card through the appropriate jacks on the back of the computer, or plug in headphones for privacy and consideration of fellow workers in an office setting.

NOTE You can listen to your music CDs, even if you do not have a sound card in your computer, by plugging your headphones or speakers in the headphone jack on the front of the CD player. The volume is then controlled using the volume control on the front of the CD player. ■

Steps

1. Click Start (or press Alt+S) and select Programs, Accessories, Multimedia, CD Player to open the CD Player program window.

2. If you have not placed an audio CD in the drive, a message, Please insert an audio compact disc, is displayed in the Title field of the dialog box. Put a CD in your CD-ROM drive, using a CD caddy if required by the CD-ROM drive.

3. Click the Play icon on the player controls toolbar to start playing the default or saved play list. The default play list for a CD includes all tracks in their original order on the CD.

4. Choose Options, Random Order, or click the Random Order icon on the menu toolbar to play the tracks specified in the play list in a random order, rather than the order of the play list.

5. Click the Stop icon on the player controls toolbar to stop playing a CD. The play list resets to the first track in the play list. To stop and resume at the point that you stopped, click the Pause icon.

NOTE If you have a multidisc CD player or more than one CD player attached to your computer (more common if you are using a SCSI interface and CD players), you can set the CD Player to play CDs in any and all of the players, one CD after another. The CDs are played in the order that the CD drives are mounted (addressed by the CD controller drivers), using the play lists set up for each disc. Click the Multidisc Play icon on the menu toolbar, or select Options, Multidisc Play from the menu in the CD Player dialog box. ▦

Audio CDs: Playing Continuously

The CD Player plays music and audio CDs as long as the program is open. You can set the player program to continue to play CDs even when the CD Player program has been closed, not just minimized.

Steps

1. Click Start (or press Alt+S) and select Programs, Accessories, Multimedia, CD Player to open the CD Player program window.

2. If you have not placed an audio CD in the drive, a message, `Please insert an audio compact disc`, is displayed in the Title field of the dialog box. Put a CD in your CD-ROM drive, using a CD caddy if required by the CD-ROM drive.

3. Click the Play icon on the player controls toolbar to start playing the default or saved play list. The default play list for a CD includes all tracks in their original order on the CD.

4. Select Options, Continuous Play, or click the Continuous Play icon on the menu toolbar to repeat the play list until you click Stop.

5. Select Options, Preferences to open the Preferences dialog box. Remove the check mark in the Stop CD Playing on Exit check box to enable the continuous playing after the CD Player is closed.

NOTE   When you select Continuous Play from the Options menu of the CD Player, the CD will continue to play even when the CD Player is closed. To stop the playback of the CD, click the Stop icon on the player controls toolbar. ▪

Audio CDs: Playing from the Desktop

It is not necessary to go through the five steps required to open the CD player and start playing a music CD. The CD Player program can be opened as easily as clicking the CD drive icon in My Computer and selecting Play.

Steps

1. Place a music CD in your CD-ROM drive, using a CD caddy if required by the CD-ROM drive.

2. Double-click My Computer and right-click the CD drive icon.

3. Select Play from the menu. The CD Player is started and placed on the taskbar.

NOTE   The Play option is shown in the CD drive submenu only when the Auto Insert Notification option is selected in the CD drive Properties dialog box opened from the Device Manager in the System program found in the Control Panel. (See also "Device Manager: Examining the Hardware in Your Computer" in the "Equipment Configuration" part of this book.) ▪

Audio CDs: Using CD Player

You can play music or audio CDs in your CD-ROM drive while you are using the computer to do your work. Use the CD Player program to play the CDs in track order or random order, or create your own play list.

NOTE An information message box is displayed with a message, There is no CD-ROM player attached to this computer. CD Player cannot start, when your CD-ROM drive is not installed or is turned off. If your CD-ROM drive is in an external case, turn it on and restart your computer. Open the Device Manager in the System program found in the Control Panel to check the configuration of the CD-ROM drive if it is installed inside your computer. (See also "Device Manager: Examining the Hardware in Your Computer" in the "Equipment Configuration" part of this book.) ■

Steps

1. Click Start (or press Alt+S) and select Programs, Accessories, Multimedia, CD Player to open the CD Player program window. If you have not placed an audio CD in the drive, a message, Please insert an audio compact disc, is displayed in the Title field of the dialog box. Put a CD in your CD-ROM drive, using a CD caddy if required by the CD-ROM drive.

2. Click the Eject icon, the last icon in the second player controls toolbar to the right of the Timer field that looks like a vertical arrowhead above an underline, to open and close the CD tray or to eject a CD caddy if used. New Artist is displayed in the Artist field when a compact disc is in the CD-ROM drive.

3. Click the Play icon, the first icon in the first player controls toolbar to the right of the Timer field that looks like an arrowhead pointing to the right, to start playing the audio CD. To see the order of the current play list, click the Track drop-down list box.

Click the Stop icon, the square icon at the end of the first player controls toolbar, to stop playing the audio CD and return the order of tracks to play to the top of the play list. Click the Pause icon, the icon with two vertical parallel lines, to pause the play at the current point of the play list. Click Play again to resume play from the point at which you clicked Pause.

4. Select Options, Continuous Play to play the tracks on the audio CD continually, repeating the play list when the end has been reached. Select Options, Random Order to play the tracks in a random order. When you select Intro Play from the Options menu, a short (10 seconds by default) introduction of each track is played in the order defined in the play list.

5. Click Options, Preferences to open the Preferences dialog box. Click the up or down arrows of the Intro Play Length (Seconds) spin box to specify how much of each track to play when the Intro Play option is checked in the Options menu. When a check mark is placed in the Stop CD Playing on Exit check box, the audio CD will stop playing when the CD Player is closed, but not when it is minimized.

NOTE You can use the Volume Control program from the Multimedia submenu in the Accessories group when you have your CD drive connected to a sound card installed in your computer. Connect the drive to the audio inputs of the sound card either through the internal connections or using a cable between the headphone jack on the CD drive and the line-in jack on the outside of the sound card (as with an external CD-ROM drive). Then, open the Volume Control and adjust the volume and balance in the Line-in or Volume Control sections. The Volume Control section controls all inputs, Line-in, Wave, and MIDI, at one time. (See also "Multimedia: Using Volume Control.")

Device Drivers: Changing

Windows 95 installs the device drivers that it thinks are most appropriate for the hardware that it identifies. Many times, Windows recognizes the manufacturer of a device, but not the model, therefore it is necessary to change the drivers manually. To do this, you open the Control Panel and open the program for that device. For example, open Modems for your faxmodem, Joystick for your game controllers, or Mouse for your pointer device.

Steps

1. Click Start (or press Alt+S) and select Settings, Control Panel, to open the Control Panel folder. Double-click the Display icon to open the Display Properties dialog box. Click the Settings tab to bring the Settings property sheet to the front.

2. Click the Change Display Type button to open the Change Display Type dialog box where you can change the adapter type or the monitor type by clicking the Change button to the right of the appropriate field. Click the Change button to the right of the Monitor Type field. If you have version B of Windows 95, see the Notes following these steps.

3. Click the Show All Devices option button to display a complete list of monitors.

4. Select the manufacturer of your monitor from the Manufacturers list box; then select the model from the Models list box and click OK. If the selected model is a green (energy conserving) compliant monitor, the check box labeled Monitor is Energy Star Compliant will be checked.

5. Click Close to return to the Display Properties dialog box. Now, select 16 Color, 256 Color, High Color (16-bit), or True Color (24-bit) from the Color Palette drop-down list box; 640 by 480 Pixels, 800 by 600 Pixels, or 1024 by 768 Pixels from the Desktop Area slide bar; and Large Fonts or Small Fonts from the Font Size drop-down list box if you have selected 800 by 600 or 1024 by 768.

MULTIMEDIA

NOTE These steps are based on Microsoft Windows 95, version 4.00.950 A. If your version of Windows 95 is different, your steps for this task will vary. To check your version of Windows, right-click the My Computer icon, choose Properties, and look at the System entry on the General page. ■

NOTE If you have version B, in the previous Step 2 click the Advanced Properties button to open the Advanced Display Properties dialog box. Click the Monitor tab to bring the Monitor property sheet to the front. To change the monitor, click the Change button. ■

NOTE The Desktop Area setting actually affects the colors that you can select; the higher the resolution, the fewer the colors that are usable. In 1024 by 768 mode, only 256 and 16 colors are applicable, in 800 by 600, you can select from High Color, 256, or 16 colors. ■

Games: Setting Up DOS Games

Windows 95 and programs written for it (or any 32-bit operating system such as Windows NT) are designed to be run at the same time as other 32-bit programs. However, Windows 3.1x programs are written for the 16-bit environment where you can have multiple programs open. But, only the program that is in front (the window that is open in front of you) is actually running; any other open programs are paused until you bring them to the front of the desktop.

Games written for Windows 95 or Windows 3.1x are easily played under Windows 95. They are designed to use the memory and other device resources that you have installed in your computer. However, if you intend to play games that are written specifically for Windows 3.1x while you are using another Windows program, there can be minor problems related to multitasking.

In addition, games that are designed to run from DOS require some special settings in Windows 95. Many of the DOS games require that you run the programs from DOS, not in a DOS window.

NOTE Windows 95 comes pre-configured for many DOS games and other program requirements. Open the file named APPS.INF, installed with Windows 95 in \WINDOWS\INF, to see if your game is listed. If you have version B of Windows 95, open the file PROGRAMS.TXT which contains information about running MS-DOS programs, as well as specific compatibility information for certain software. ■

Steps

1. Open the folders and locate the game program. Right-click the program icon and select Properties to open the program's Properties dialog box.

2. Click the Program tab to bring the Program property sheet to the front. Click the Advanced button to open the Advanced Program Settings dialog box where you customize the settings for the DOS session.

3. Click the MS-DOS Mode check box, and then select the Specify a New MS-DOS Configuration option button.

4. Compare the current settings in the CONFIG.SYS for MS-DOS Mode list box to the settings specified in the game program manual, making any changes as needed. Then, compare the current settings in the AUTOEXEC.BAT for MS-DOS Mode list box to the settings in the manual, making any changes as needed.

5. Click the Configuration button to open the Select MS-DOS Configuration Options. Click the check box to the left of each of the possible options: *EMS* (Expanded Memory Specification), Mouse, Disk Cache, MS-DOS Command Line Editor (Doskey), and Direct Disk Access, to enable the option while running the game from DOS. Click OK in each of the dialog boxes to accept the changes and finally return to the desktop.

The next time you run the game from Windows 95, the game will use these settings when DOS is started.

Joysticks: Calibrating in Windows 95

There are many brands and types of joysticks and other game
controllers in use with DOS and Windows games. Windows 95
provides the Joystick control panel program to define and
configure your joystick for the best action possible.

Steps

1. Click Start (or press Alt+S) and select Settings, Control
    Panel. Double-click the Joystick icon to open the Joystick
    Properties dialog box.

2. Select the joystick to be calibrated from the Current
    Joystick drop-down list box, if you have more than one
    joystick installed.

3. Select the type of joystick from the Joystick Selection
    drop-down list box, or select Custom from the list box to
    define another type of game controller.

4. Click the Test button to open the Joystick Test dialog
    box where you test the Joystick, Throttle, Rudder, Button
    1, and Button 2 controls, clicking OK to return to the
    Joystick Properties dialog box.

5. Click the Calibrate button to further configure the game
    controller/joystick. Click OK when you are satisfied with
    the calibration of the joystick, and click OK again in the
    Joystick Properties dialog box to apply the changes and
    return to the desktop.

NOTE   If you have problems with the game controller, use the
Device Manager in the System program found in the Control
Panel to check the input range of the game port driver. It is
necessary that the input range for the game port driver be set to
0201-0201. ▓

Multimedia: Linking Media Clips

Linking a clip to a document or other file, rather than embedding the clip, saves space in the file. If you are working in an
office setting and distributing the document with the link over

a network, the recipients will only receive the file, leaving the clip on your computer to be accessed when the recipients click the link icons in their copies of the document.

Steps

1. Click Start (or press Alt+S) and select Find, Files Or Folders to open the Find: Files dialog box. Type ***.WAV** in the Named field and click the Find Now button. Double-click The Microsoft Sound name in the list box at the bottom of the Find: Files dialog box. When the Open With dialog box opens, asking you to Click the program you want to use to open the file, double-click mplayer, the Media Player.

2. Choose Edit, Selection. Click the All option button and click OK to return to the Media Player. Choose Edit, Copy Object to copy the .WAV clip to the Windows Clipboard.

3. Click Start (or press Alt+S) and select Programs, Accessories, WordPad to create a document in the WordPad program shipped with Windows 95.

4. Select Edit, Paste to embed the .WAV clip in the document.

Multimedia: Using Media Player to Add Music to a Document

Multimedia uses the prefix multi because there can be many different components used in creating multimedia files. The Multimedia program opened from the Control Panel is used to customize the basic features of multimedia devices such as selecting the devices and drivers to use, setting the default volume for the devices, selecting the quality of audio recordings (affecting not just the sound quality, but also the amount of hard drive space used to save recordings), and so on.

The Media Player is used to play audio and music CDs, as well as audio, video, and animation files not necessarily found on a

CD. The Media Player is also used to edit and copy audio, video, and animation clips, embedding or linking them into documents and other files.

NOTE   The Media Player only recognizes media placed in the first CD-ROM drive if you have more than one attached to your computer, unlike the CD Player used for just music CDs. ▓

TIP   Use the Media Player instead of the CD Player to play music CDs once you have created your play lists. The Media Player performs all of the functions of the CD Player, other than creating and editing play lists, and gives you the means to capture clips for use in other programs.

Steps

1. Click Start (or press Alt+S) and select Programs, Accessories, Multimedia, Media Player to open the Media Player program window.

2. Select Device to open the Device menu. Select ActiveMovie, Video for Windows, Sound, MIDI Sequencer, or CD Audio (shown in the menu if you do not have CD Player already open) to indicate the type of media you want to work with. If you select CD Audio, click the Play icon (the arrowhead pointing to the right) from the media controls toolbar to start playing a music CD. Click the Pause or Stop icon to stop playing.

3. Click the Start Selection icon, an arrowhead pointing down with a horizontal I underneath. Click the End Selection icon, an arrowhead pointing up with a horizontal I underneath, to complete the selection. Select Edit, Copy Object to copy the selection to the Windows Clipboard.

4. Click Start (or press Alt+S) and select Programs, Accessories, WordPad to open the WordPad program window. Enter any text that you want and move the cursor to the point where you want to embed the music

clip. Select Edit, Paste to embed it in the WordPad document. The clip can then be started by double-clicking the embedded icon. (See also "Sound: Adding Sound Effects to a Document" in this part and "Sharing: Using Object Linking and Embedding (OLE)" in the "Applications and Accessories" part of this book.)

It is also important to review and modify the properties of any multimedia programs that may have been added to the Control Panel during installation, such as QuickTime for Windows and the devices in the System program under Device Manager, to get the most out of your equipment. (See also "Device Manager: Examining the Hardware in Your Computer" in the "Equipment Configuration" part of this book.)

Multimedia: Using Volume Control

The Volume Control tool, found in the Multimedia group on the Accessories menu, is used to adjust the volume and balance of sound being recorded and played back. You can open the Volume Control dialog box from any of the programs that play or record audio and music, or from the taskbar.

The use of all of the hardware options for multimedia can cause problems that you do not realize. Some problems can be fixed using the Device Manager in the System program on the Control Panel, but some problems are less obvious because they may be related to the hardware wiring.

NOTE If Volume Control is not in the Mulitimedia group of the Accessories menu, open the Control Panel and double-click Add/Remove Programs. Select the Windows Setup tab and highlight Multimedia in the Components list box. With Multimedia highlighted, click the Details button, scroll to the bottom of the Components list box in the Multimedia dialog box, and locate Volume Control. If Volume Control does not have a check mark in the check box to the left, check the box and close the dialog boxes. Setup will prompt you for your Windows 95 CD or diskettes and will install Volume Control on your hard drive, adding it to the Accessories menu. ■

To open the Volume Control program from any of the following programs, use the indicated menu steps:

- **CD Player:** Select View, Volume Control.
- **Media Player:** Select Device, Volume Control.
- **Taskbar:** Right-click the Volume Control icon (a speaker in the taskbar) and select Open Volume Controls.

Steps

1. Click Start (or press Alt+S) and select Programs, Accessories, Multimedia, Volume Control to open the Volume Control dialog box.

2. Select Options, Properties to open the Properties dialog box. Select either the Playback, Recording, or Other option button in the Adjust Volume For group to determine what type of devices you want to change. Then, place a check mark in the check box next to the desired device(s) in the Show the Following Volume Controls group immediately below. Click OK to return to the Volume Control dialog box.

3. Click the vertical bar in the appropriate Volume control to raise or lower the volume of the desired device.

4. Click to the left or right of the Balance pointer to adjust the balance between your two channels.

5. Choose Options, Exit to close the Volume Control dialog box and return to the desktop.

To set both Playback and Recording, repeat the previous steps, first selecting Playback in the Properties dialog box and making the adjustments, then selecting Recording and making the recording adjustments.

When you select Playback in the Properties dialog box, you check the check boxes to the left of Volume Control, Line-In, Wave, and MIDI in the Show the Following Volume Controls list box to adjust the checked devices. Select Recording and check the check boxes next to Line-In and Microphone to adjust the selected devices. If you select the Other option in the Properties dialog box, select the other type of controls in the drop-down list box to the right of Other. Then check the devices to be adjusted in the list box below.

NOTE   To turn off the sound for all devices, place a check mark in the Mute All check box by clicking the box in the Volume Control dialog box. To mute only specific displayed devices, place a check mark in the Mute check box of the specific device control. ■

TROUBLESHOOTING   The volume control for Line-In is too loud at the next-to-mute setting. An external CD player is connected from its headphone jack to the Line-In plug on the sound card. Turn down the volume control on the external CD player, then adjust the volume control for the Line-In in the Volume Control program.

No matter how loud I adjust the Line-In volume control, I am getting no sound out of my sound card. Check that your headphones or speakers are plugged in to the right jack on the sound card. Check the Device Manager in the System program, opened from the Control Panel, to make sure that the sound card is functioning properly. Also, open the Volume Control program, choose Options, Properties and select the Playback option button from the Adjust Volume For group. Make sure that there is a check mark in the Volume Control check box at the bottom of the dialog box. Then make sure that the Mute All check box is not checked.

Sound: Adding Sound Effects to a Document

Whether you are using the Sound Recorder installed with Windows 95 or a third-party recording program, the saved sound clip can be placed in documents, spreadsheets, database records, or just about any other Windows program data file for playback. The recording can be made from a music CD, a microphone, or any other device connected to the sound card in your PC.

The sound clip, or object in Windows parlance, can be linked or embedded (OLE, Object Linking/Embedding) in documents. A linked object remains on the original hard drive and is accessed (over a network in an office setting if the file is sent to a colleague over the network) when the sound icon in the document is clicked. An embedded object is actually included in the file and is also accessed when the icon is clicked. Embed a clip when the document is going to be opened on a computer that is not connected in any way to the computer that created and is storing the clip. (See also "Sharing: Using Object Linking and Embedding (OLE)" in the "Applications and Accessories" part of this book.)

CAUTION   It is very important to review the sound properties that you have selected for recording. If you have decided to record at CD Quality using 44,100 Hz, 16 Bit Stereo, the recording will use 172K of hard drive space for every second of recording. A 60-second recording, therefore, uses 10M of space.

The clips can be added to just about any document created by a Windows-compatible program. In the following example, use the WordPad program included with Windows 95, or your favorite program. The steps are the same; part of the concept of Common User Access (CUA) is that learning different Windows programs can be easy because the common keystrokes are the same. The example assumes that you have already made a recording as described in the steps in the task "Sound: Using Sound Recorder."

Steps

1. Click Start (or press Alt+S) and select Programs, Accessories, WordPad to open the WordPad program window.

2. Enter some text and move the cursor to the point where you want to insert the sound clip object. Choose Insert, Object. Select the Create From File option and click the

Browse button to open the Browse window. Move to the folder where the sound clip file is saved and double-click the file name. The file name (with the full path) is displayed in the File field.

3. To place a link to the clip in the document, click the Link check box and click OK; otherwise, just click OK to embed the clip and return to the WordPad window. If you did not check the Link check box, you may not return to WordPad immediately if the sound clip file is large. The file is being inserted in the document, also increasing the document file size.

4. The clip can be easily removed from the document by choosing Edit, Undo before you make any other changes, or by clicking the sound clip icon, opening a frame around the clip, and pressing Delete.

5. Double-click the sound clip icon to hear the recording.

To control the playback volume, right-click the Volume Control icon on the taskbar and select Volume Controls from the menu. In the Volume Control window, adjust the Volume and Balance controls for Wave output. As the recording is being played, a thermometer display to the right of the Volume control will reflect the loudness of the original recording.

If the Wave volume control is not shown in the Volume Control window, select Options, Properties to open the Properties window for the Volume Control program. Select the Playback option in the Adjust Volume For group in the Properties window, check the Wave check box in the Show the Following Volume Controls, and click the OK button to return to the Volume Control where you can now adjust the volume for the recording.

Sound: Customizing Windows 95 Event Sounds

Windows uses sounds for more than just games. Windows 95 has numerous events that can have custom sound clips (.WAV files) attached to the events that play when the event is executed. Many programs not currently listed will add their events to the list.

The following table shows the Windows programs and the events within these programs that are installed with Windows 95 and can have sound clips attached.

Events in Windows Programs that Can Have Sound Clips	
Program	**Event**
Windows	Asterisk
	Close Program
	Critical Stop
	Default Sound
	Exclamation
	Exit Windows *
	Maximize
	Menu Command
	Menu Popup
	Minimize
	New Mail Notification
	Open Program
	Program Error
	Question
	Restore Down
	Restore Up
	Start Windows *
Windows Explorer	Empty Recycle Bin
Sound Recorder	Close Program
	Open Program

Program	Event
Media Player	Close Program
	Open Program
	Microsoft NetMeeting**
	Person Joins
	Person Leaves
	Receive Call
	Receive Request to Join

indicates an event that has a predefined sound clip when installed.

** *indicates a program and events included in version B of Windows 95.*

The sound clip, a .WAV file, is played back at any time the event occurs, such as when Windows closes. By default, two Windows events, Exit Windows and Start Windows, are assigned The Microsoft Sound. You pick a .WAV file from any location on your system, as long as the file is accessible when the event occurs. The Preview feature lets you try a .WAV clip before applying it to an event.

The Sounds Properties program also allows you to group the events together in sound schemes, simplifying changes to common events, as you group them. Save the schemes or delete them with the click of the button. The default sound scheme is Windows Default. To remove all event sound definitions, select No Sounds in the Schemes drop-down list box.

NOTE All .WAV files located in the folder selected in the Browse dialog box are selectable from the Name drop-down list box. The default options in the list box are (None) and The Microsoft Sound, but if a folder other than \WINDOWS\MEDIA is selected, The Microsoft Sound is removed from the list until the home folder is selected again. ▨

Steps

1. Click Start (or press Alt+S) and select Settings, Control Panel. Double-click the Sounds icon to open the Sounds Properties dialog box with Windows highlighted in the Events list box.

2. Press O (the letter, not a zero) to move to the first Open Program event in the list box. (If you press O again, the focus (highlight) moves to the next event that starts with an O.) (None) is the default sound selection in the Name field. Click the Browse button to open the Browse for Open Program Sound (the highlighted event) dialog box.

3. Move to the folder that contains your .WAV files (\SNDSYS\SOUNDS if you have a Microsoft Sound System card installed) and highlight the file name. Click the Preview Play button, the arrowhead pointing to the right, in the bottom-right corner of the dialog box to listen to the sound clip. Click OK to select the sound clip and return to the Sounds Properties dialog box.

4. Click the Save As button in the Schemes group to save the new event sound definition as a new sound scheme. Highlight any scheme other than No Sounds or Windows Default, and click the Delete button to remove the scheme from the list.

Any copyright or similar information embedded in the header of the sound clip is displayed when you highlight a sound clip in the Name field and click the Details button, along with Media Length of the clip in seconds and the Audio Format that it was recorded in.

NOTE Use the WAVE Balance and Volume control in the Volume Control dialog box to control the balance and volume of the event sound clips (as a whole, not individually). Placing a check mark in the Wave Mute check box disables the playback of all event sounds. ▪

Sound: Playing a Media File

The Media Player is designed to play any type of media file (whether it is audio, MIDI, or video), and select and cut portions to the Windows Clipboard. Media clips that are copied to the Clipboard can then be included in documents, spreadsheets, other files, or other media clips.

Steps

1. Click Start (or press Alt+S) and select Programs, Accessories, Multimedia, Media Player to open the Media Player program window.

2. Choose Device, Sound to open the Open (file) dialog box. Move to the folder where the sound clip file is located and double-click the file name, such as The Microsoft Sound located in the \WINDOWS\MEDIA folder, a 6.12-second recording played by default at the startup of Windows 95.

3. Click the Play button, an arrowhead pointing to the right, on the controls toolbar at the bottom of the window to play the clip. The Start button changes to a Pause button until the end of the clip is reached, or the Pause or Stop button is pressed.

4. The elapsed time that the clip has played is displayed in the small window to the right of the controls toolbar.

5. Choose Edit, Selection to select a portion of the clip, and then select Edit, Copy Object to copy the selected range to the Windows Clipboard.

NOTE   You can set the media file to continually repeat, and set other options such as Place a Border Around Object and Play in Client Document, by choosing Edit, Options and selecting the settings that you want in the Options dialog box.

MULTIMEDIA

Sound: Using MIDI and .WAV Sound Files

Windows multimedia programs can work with CD audio (music CDs), sound (.WAV), or MIDI (.MID) files, recording and playing back the sound clips. Each type of sound clip can also be linked or embedded in documents, spreadsheets, and other types of files.

The CD Player is used to play audio or music CDs only. The Sound Recorder can record from any source, Line-In or MIDI, but it saves the recordings only in .WAV format. Use the Media Player to get the most versatility in creating and playing back multimedia (the most versatility of the bundled Windows 95 multimedia tools, not including third-party programs). The Volume Control works with any of these Windows programs.

The Media Player allows you to record and play back from audio, CD, MIDI, video sources, and saved files.

Steps

1. Select a section of the recording and choose Edit, Copy to place the section in the Windows Clipboard.

2. Open your document or other file in its program and choose Edit, Paste to place the object in the file.

Sound: Using Sound Recorder

The Sound Recorder, installed with Windows 95, is your channel for creating the audio portion of your own multimedia clips. Using the Sound Recorder, located in the Multimedia portion of the Accessories menu, you can capture sound clips from any type of sound device connected to the sound card in your computer, including CDs, video tapes, and a microphone.

Sound clips, or bites, can then be used in the development of, and subsequent recording to, your own CD. Or, they can be linked to or embedded in documents and files that you want to distribute to friends and colleagues. While the Sound Recorder is not as full-featured as a commercial product, you can still do a very good job of creating your own clips.

CAUTION   It is very important to review the sound properties that you have selected for recording. If you have decided to record at CD Quality using 44,100 Hz, 16 Bit Stereo, the recording will use 172K of hard drive space for every second of recording.

A 60-second recording, therefore, uses 10M of space. At least the size of hard drives has come up (a typical hard drive in a new system is 1.2G), while the price has dropped (a 10M hard drive purchased in 1986 cost $900, by the end of 1996, a 1.2G hard drive cost less than $200).

Steps

1. Click Start (or press Alt+S) and select Programs, Accessories, Multimedia, Sound Recorder to open the Sound Recorder program window.

2. Choose File, Properties, select Recording Formats from the Choose From drop-down list box in the Properties for Sound dialog box, and click the Convert Now button to the right of the list box. Review and change, if you need to, the settings for quality in the Name drop-down list box and recording quality in the Attributes drop-down list box. Click the OK buttons to close the Sound Selection and Properties for Sound dialog boxes and return to the Sound Recorder.

3. Using a microphone attached to the appropriate jack on your sound card, record a message by clicking the red Record button at the bottom-right corner of the recorder. As the recording is happening, you will notice that a green bar is displayed and will continually expand and contract in the window at the center of the recorder window. This is the visual wave display that reflects the volume and intensity of the recording. Click the black square Stop button to the left of the Record button.

4. Click the Seek to Start button, the double arrowheads pointing to the left, to return to the start of the recording. Click the Play button to play your recording.

MULTIMEDIA

5. To change or add effects to your recording, choose Effects from the Sound Recorder menu and select one of the menu options: Increase Volume (by 25%), Decrease Volume, Increase Speed (by 100%), Decrease Speed, Add Echo, or Reverse. Changes can be changed back to the immediately previous setting (unless you have done a File, Save) by selecting File, Revert. Choose File, Save to save the clip for use in a multimedia creation or other application.

Once you have recorded a sound clip, you are only limited by your own imagination as to how to use it.

Video: Apple's QuickTime for Windows

QuickTime for Windows 95, originally developed at Apple Corp. for the Macintosh, is one of the most common driver sets used for multimedia video clips. When a video clip is created for QuickTime, it can be viewed on both Windows and Macintosh computers, reducing the production cost while increasing the market. QuickTime for Windows 95 is available on the Internet at **http://quicktime.apple.com/sw**.

Steps

1. Using your Internet account, go to **quicktime.apple.com/sw** and download the QuickTime for Windows drivers (in zipped form). When the transfer is finished, close your browser and dialer. Depending on the speed of your modem or other connection, the download can take several hours.

2. Open the folder that the zipped file was downloaded to and double-click the file icon. A DOS window is opened and the uncompressed file, QT32INST.EXE, is extracted. Close the DOS windows when the extraction is finished.

3. Click Start (or press Alt+S) and select Settings, Control Panel, then double-click the Add/Remove Programs icon. Click the Install button in the Install/Uninstall sheet of the Add/Remove Programs Properties dialog box.

4. Click Next and then the Browse button. Move to the appropriate folder where QT32INST.EXE is located and double-click the file. Click Finish in the Run Installation Program window.

5. Click the Agree button in the software license declaration if you agree to the conditions of the license and want to continue the installation. Click Install in the Begin Install dialog box; and click Start to check for a previous version of the QuickTime drivers. Click the Install button in the Complete Install window to complete the installation. A sample movie is included that you can preview when the installation is finished.

When the installation is finished, a new folder has been created, QuickTime for Windows, in the \WINDOWS\START MENU\PROGRAMS folder with five files: Movie Player 32-bit, Picture Viewer 32-bit, QuickTime Read Me 32-bit,Reinstall QuickTime 32-bit, and Uninstall QuickTime 32-bit. The QuickTime folder is also placed in the Start menu under Programs during the installation.

A new control panel, QuickTime 32, is added to the Control Panel as part of the installation. The panel displays information for the status of your computer and the hardware being used by QuickTime for Windows.

NOTE Use the Add/Remove Programs control in the Control Panel to install the program files. All files are then registered and can be easily removed at a later time. ■

Video: Using Full-Motion Video

Full-motion videos are just about the most system-intensive process that you can put your computer through if you want to have real video, meaning flicker-free. The first most important component to have is a fast hard drive. The other component that can affect the recording and playback of full-motion video is the sound card.

Hard drives that use a SCSI (Small Computer Systems Interface) interface, are the fastest type of drive possible, making for a more even transfer of video data during capture and playback. Look for a hard drive that lists a high rotation speed, such as 7200 RPM, and uses at least a SCSI-2 interface.

When considering a sound card to use, look for a card that uses true 16-bit DMA (Dynamic Memory Addressing), rather than 8-bit DMA, sometimes found in a 16-bit sound card. The memory addressing uses processor time, thereby affecting the video capture.

Steps

1. Always defragment the hard drive that you intend to capture video to before starting the capture.

2. Update your video card drivers to the most current version of Windows 95.

   Many drivers were written before Windows 95 came on the market and are not necessarily as well tuned to the 95 system.

3. Use the highest quality cables possible between the video capture board and the video input device, whether a VCR, video camera, and so on, to ensure the highest quality image.

4. Use a disk utility to order your files on the hard drive, with the video data files located closer to the outside of the drive where access is faster because the data is not compressed (whereas data on inner tracks is compressed).

5. Use the Media Player to play your videos.

(See also "Video: Using Video for Windows 95.")

Video: Using Video for Windows 95

Multimedia includes movieCDs and full-motion videos. These require the use of video driver programs such as QuickTime for Windows and Video for Windows. If a video or movieCD, such as The Gate to the Mind's Eye from Sirius, uses Video for Windows, the publisher includes the runtime version with the program files. When you first start the video, the program checks your system to determine if Video for Windows is present and installs it for you if it is not found.

Video for Windows is also bundled with expansion boards that you can add to your system for use in creating your own video events, such as the Video Blaster from Creative Labs. The bundled version installs additional programs, Media Player, VidCap, and VidEdit, in a new folder named Video for Windows, accessible from the Start menu under Programs. Additional editing programs, BitEdit, PalEdit, and WaveEdit, are placed in a new folder, Multimedia Data Tools. Program shortcuts are also placed in the Multimedia Data Tools folder under Programs in the Start menu.

Steps

1. Insert the movieCD in your CD drive and double-click the icon on the desktop.

2. The InstallShield Wizard is loaded if Video for Windows is not found on your computer, and the Runtime version of Video for Windows is installed. Then, the movie software (The Motion Pixels Movie Player software if you are preparing to view the Gate to the Mind from Sirius) is installed, creating a new folder with the program files, and adding the folder to the Programs menu.

3. The movieCD is then played.

The full version of Video for Windows lets you edit the .AVI and the .WAV files of existing and new videos, while the Runtime version can only view existing videos.

NOTE It is necessary to check the version and date of the Media Player program shipped with the full version Video for Windows software and use the newer version. The shipped version uses the same .INI file as the Media Player shipped with Windows 95, and either program may make changes that are incompatible for the other version. However, there are no additional features in the .VFW version.

Communications

During the last couple of decades, the computer communications market has exploded. You now have the ability to exchange files with a computer on the other side of the world; send a message to several people at once without scheduling a meeting; and receive, read, and send a fax without ever touching a piece of fax paper.

Then there's the Internet, which lets you talk to millions of computers across the world. You can find information on the latest bills in congress without leaving the office; communicate in real time with your corespondent in Europe without making a phone call; or spend the day at a shopping mall without leaving your home.

Windows 95 puts all the power of this new form of communication at your fingertips with its built-in tools. You can use HyperTerminal to connect to Bulletin Board Systems; Microsoft Fax to send and receive faxes; Microsoft Messaging System (also known as Microsoft Exchange) to send and receive electronic mail; and Internet Explorer to browse the World Wide Web. Windows 95 even provides access to the Microsoft Network (MSN) for Internet access if you aren't already on the Internet.

Bulletin Boards: Accessing

Bulletin Board Systems, or BBSs, have been meeting grounds for computer users since the first days of computer communication. Most BBSs offer mail, message groups, and interesting files. Many companies have bulletin boards to provide support and make company bulletins available.

Steps

1. Open the HyperTerminal folder by choosing Start, Programs, Accessories, HyperTerminal.

2. Double-click the Hypertrm.exe icon. Double check the settings and click Connect.

3. Wait for the connection to be established and enter your user name and password when (if) prompted.

 TIP If you haven't previously connected to the bulletin board, create a connection according to the instructions in "HyperTerminal: Configuring."

Dial-Up Networking: Connecting

Dial-up networking enables you to connect to a network without a physical connection to the network. For example, you can use dial-up networking to connect to the largest network around (the Internet), or you could use it on your home PC to connect to your network at work. With dial-up networking you can use any of the network, even though you are not plugged directly into the network.

Steps

1. Open the Dial-Up Networking folder by choosing Start, Programs, Accessories, Dial-Up Networking.

2. Double-click the connection you want to make.

3. By default, your dialing/logon information is displayed. Double check all the settings and click the Connect button.

Dial-Up Networking: Setting Up

Dial-up networking enables you to connect to a network without a physical connection to the network. Before hooking up to the Internet or your company network, you need to create a dial-up networking connection. The connection stores things like the phone number, your user name, password, and the type of network you'll access. Creating a dial-up networking connection is a simple matter of answering some questions for the Add Connection Wizard.

Steps

1. Open the Dial-Up Networking folder by choosing Start, Programs, Accessories, Dial-Up Networking. Double-click the Make New Connection icon.

2. Read each Wizard screen and provide the necessary information, then click the Next button. Once the Wizard has all the information it needs to create your connection, you will see a Finish button. Click the Finish button to complete the dial-up networking connection setup.

TIP If you realize you made a mistake when providing the Wizard information, you can use the Back button to return to a previous screen.

HyperTerminal: Configuring

HyperTerminal allows you to connect to a variety of different computers, and saves each connection separately so you don't have to change settings for every connection.

Steps

1. Open HyperTerminal by choosing Start, Programs, Accessories, HyperTerminal. Start HyperTerminal by double-clicking the HyperTerminal icon.

2. In the first dialog box, enter a name for this connection and choose an icon. Click the OK button.

3. In the next Phone Number dialog box, provide the dialing information, as well as the modem you want to use, in the Connect Using box. Click the OK button.

5. In the Connect dialog box, verify the Your Location combo box, then click the Dial button.

TIP If your modem isn't listed, you need to cancel and go to the sections "Modem: Installing Legacy" or "Modem: Installing Plug and Play" in the "Equipment Configuration" part of this book.

COMMUNICATIONS

HyperTerminal: Connecting

HyperTerminal allows you to connect to a variety of different computers. Once connected, you can transfer files, leave messages, and perform other tasks depending on the system.

Steps

1. Open HyperTerminal by choosing Start, Programs, Accessories, HyperTerminal.

2. Locate the connection you want to make, then double-click its icon. In the Connect dialog box, check the Your Location box then click the Dial button.

   If you haven't created a connection for the site, follow the instructions in the task "HyperTerminal: Configuring."

HyperTerminal: Exchanging Files

With HyperTerminal you can connect to another computer and upload (send) a file or download (receive) a file. This makes sharing information across the world quick and easy.

Steps

1. Connect to the location where you want to exchange files according to the instructions in the task "HyperTerminal: Connecting."

2. If you are receiving a file, instruct the other side to send the file. Choose Transfer, Receive File. Choose the directory where you want the file to be stored, choose the *file transfer protocol* you want to use, and click the Receive button.

3. If you are sending a file, instruct the other side to wait for a file. Choose Transfer, Send File. Select the file you want to send, choose the file transfer protocol you want to use, and click the Send button.

 TIP If you are confused about which protocol is best, ZModem offers a good combination of speed and reliability. Remember, however, that your protocol and the other side's protocol must match for the transfer to complete successfully.

Internet: Configuring Windows Internet Mail

Before you can use Microsoft's Exchange to retrieve and send your Internet mail messages, it must be installed and configured properly. This is a simple matter of adding an additional service, and answering the questions when prompted.

NOTE Version A of Windows 95 shipped with a universal mail client called Exchange. Later, in version B, Microsoft decided to change the name of the "free" version to Windows Messaging System, reserving the name Exchange for the client that ships with their Exchange Server product. ■

Steps

1. Open the Control Panel by choosing Start, Settings, Control Panel. Double-click the Mail icon.

2. If you do not have Internet Mail in your list of mail services, click the Add button. Choose Internet Mail and click OK. Simply fill in the information as provided by your Interent Sevice Provider. You may need your Windows 95 installation CD or disks to complete the installation of Internet Mail.

3. If you have the Internet Mail service installed but need to change a setting, select it from your list of services and click the Properties button. Make the desired changes and click the OK button until you are returned to the Control Panel.

Internet: Connecting from a LAN

The Internet runs on a networking protocol called TCP/IP. This same protocol can also run on a Local Area Network (*LAN*) in a company environment, to provide many people Internet access. If your company provides Internet access in this manner, then your job configuring Internet Explorer is a simple one because your network administrator took care of most of the configuration for you already.

COMMUNICATIONS

TIP Use Ping at the DOS prompt to test if you have an active Internet connection. (See "Internet: Using Ping" for more help.)

(For help on configuring your Windows 95 workstation for TCP/IP networking, see the "Networking" part of this book.)

Steps

1. Right-click the Internet icon on your desktop, and choose Properties.

2. Select the Connection tab and uncheck the Connect to the Internet as Needed box in the Dialing section. This will prevent Windows 95 from trying to use dial-up networking to make your Internet connection, and use your current LAN access.

3. If your company uses a Proxy server to access the Internet, check Connect Through a Proxy Server and click the Settings button. If you are not sure, leave it blank and click OK. If you are able to connect to a Web site, you didn't need it; if not, you need to contact your network administrator.

4. Enter your Proxy server information and click OK. If you do not know this information, contact your network administrator.

5. Click OK to save your settings, and you are ready to surf the Web.

Internet: Connecting to Your Internet Service Provider

Before you can "surf the Web," you must be able to connect your computer to the Internet. *Internet Service Provider*s (*ISP*s) give you this access (for a fee).

Steps

1. Open Dial-Up Networking by choosing Start, Programs, Accessories, Dial-Up Networking. Double-click your Internet Service Provider connection icon. If you do not have an icon for your Internet Service Provider, see the

instructions in the task "Dial-Up Networking: Setting Up."

2. Double check the settings and click the Connect button.

3. Supply a user name or password as necessary.

NOTE Software provided by some ISPs may place a new menu in the <u>P</u>rograms menu, which contains a dial-up connection. ■

Internet: Creating Your Own Web Pages

Not only can you find a lot of great information on the World Wide Web, you can also put out your own pages for other Internet users to access. This is a great way to advertise your business, notify the public of an event, publish political viewpoints, or just have fun.

Steps

1. Start a text or HTML editor, and then type the proper HTML code for your page.

2. Save the text file as an *.HTM file or *.HTML file.

3. Start Microsoft Internet Explorer and choose <u>F</u>ile, <u>O</u>pen. Click the <u>B</u>rowse button and select your file.

NOTE In order for your Web pages to be available for other Internet users to access, they must be placed on a *Web server*. If you are using a Dial-Up account, this means you have to configure your Web server software each time you connect to your ISP. In addition, your Web pages will only be available to the public while you are actually connected to your ISP. Many ISPs, however, will put your Web pages on their own Web server, which is available at all times. ■

TIP Writing Web pages in straight HTML text can be tedious and challenging. You can purchase or download a variety of HTML tools to make writing your Web page as easy as using a word processor. For more information use your *Web browser*'s Search utility to locate HTML editors.

TIP   If you are having difficulty figuring out what the HTML code should be to make your page look correct, try browsing through the Web for a page that is formatted similar to what you want. Then, you can view the source for that page to figure out what you need to do with your own code. (See "Internet Explorer 3.0: Viewing an HTML Source.")

Internet: Setting Control Panel Options

Everyone uses the Internet in different ways and for different reasons. The Internet options in the Control Panel let you decide how you want your Internet connection to work.

Steps

1. Open the Control panel by choosing Start, Settings, Control Panel. Double-click the Internet icon.

2. From here you can configure Internet Explorer options, as well as general settings like your default Internet Dial-Up networking connection. Choose the tab with the settings you want to change. Make the appropriate changes and click the OK button.

(See also "Internet Explorer 3.0: Configuring")

Internet: Using FTP

FTP stands for *File Transfer Protocol*, the set of rules that governs the transfer of a file from one location on the Internet to another. FTP clients are applications that make transferring files from one location to another simple. Windows 95 has a basic FTP client you may use.

Steps

1. Establish an Internet Connection either over a *LAN* or with an *ISP*.

2. Open an MS-DOS prompt by choosing Start, Programs, MS-DOS Prompt. Connect to an FTP server by typing **ftp <server name or IP address>**. Enter a user name and password when prompted.

3. Many FTP servers are *UNIX* machines so you can change directories with the cd command and find the current directory with the pwd command. For a list of files in the current directory, you can use the ls command.

4. Unless you are transferring a strictly ASCII text file, enter the command **binary** at the prompt to set the transfer mode.

   If you want to upload a file, change directories on the remote server until you find the directory you want to copy the file(s) into. Then type **put <directory/ filename>** and press Enter.

   If you want to download a file, change directories until you find the file you want. Then type **get <filename>** and press Enter.

5. When you are through, type quit to exit FTP.

TIP   Windows 95's FTP client is command-line or text-based, which is not user-friendly or intuitive. For easier use, invoke the Search feature on your *Web browser* and look for an FTP client that is Windows-based. These FTP clients are much easier to use.

NOTE   Many public servers do not require that you have a specific logon name or password. You can usually log on as anonymous and use your e-mail address as a password. Most Windows FTP clients will have a check box or button you can use for anonymous logon so that you don't have to enter the name and password yourself.

TROUBLESHOOTING   **I'm positive I typed the correct address for an FTP server and that the user name and password are correct. The connection seems to go through, but I never even see a directory listing for the FTP server.** If you access the Internet from work, your company may have a firewall to secure the company's network from outside interference. Some firewalls, however, block incoming FTP information.

continues

continued

> You can still use your FTP client from behind a firewall if your client supports passive mode. Check your client's connection options (Help is a really quick way to find these) to see if it supports passive mode. If it doesn't, get another FTP client.

Internet: Using Internet News to View UseNet Newsgroups

One large attraction of the Internet is that you can "meet" people across the world and discuss common interests. UseNet News is one of the best ways to do just that. UseNet is made up of message areas named for the subject of the articles within the message area. Users can find an appealing message area and read and respond to the current articles or create a new article. Any response or new article will be available for anyone else on the Internet to read and respond to.

This section describes the use of Microsoft's simple Internet News application that comes with Windows 95 version B and Internet Explorer 3, complete install. If you are using another news application (NNTP or Network News Transfer Protocol), some of the general concepts still apply.

Steps

1. Establish an Internet connection either over a *LAN* or with an *ISP*. Start Microsoft's InternetNews program by clicking Start, Programs, Internet News.

2. When started for the first time, a wizard will prompt you for the information provided to you from your ISP to connect to a UseNet. Usually, it is something like this: **nntp.isp.com.**, where isp is your Internet Service Provider.

   Initially, you will want to download a list of all the newsgroups available on the news server. This could take some time since most servers have more than 15,000 newsgroups.

3. To find a newsgroup(s) that you like and download the current messages for that group(s), click the Newsgroups button on the toolbar. In the Display Newsgroups that Contain field, type in a keyword that might be in the name of the group you are looking for, like Windows.

4. A list of all the newsgroups that contain your keyword will display. Double-clicking a newsgroup will subscribe you to that group. Clicking the Go To button will take you into the group and display the first 300 message headers.

5. You can read any article by double-clicking its icon. If you want to respond to the article, click the Reply button on your toolbar. You may also forward a news article to another newsgroup or an individual via e-mail; simply click the Forward button on your toolbar.

6. If you want to create a new message in the group you are currently in, click the New Message button on your toolbar. Enter the newsgroup(s) you want the article posted to, enter a subject for your article, type your article, and click the Post Message button on the toolbar.

WARNING Newsgroups users have a strict code of ethics that you don't want to violate. If you are unfamiliar with newsgroups, you may want to just read for a while before you start posting your own articles. Specifically, read articles posted in the news.admin groups. If you are going to post, remember that advertising can only be done in the context of the topic (if in doubt don't do it) and typing in UPPERCASE is reserved for shouting.

TIP If you are charged long distance or billed for cumulative Internet access time, choose a news client that lets you disconnect from the Internet while your read and write news articles. Then, you only need to connect to download new articles and upload articles you want to post.

COMMUNICATIONS

Internet: Using MS Internet Mail

The Internet has made keeping in touch with people across
the world simple and affordable. You can send anyone on the
Internet anywhere in the world an almost instantaneous electronic message. If the recipient of your e-mail is around when
your message arrives, you may also get an instantaneous response.

This section describes the use of Microsoft's simple Internet
Mail application that comes with Windows 95 version B and
Internet Explorer 3, complete install. If you are using another
mail application, some of the general concepts still apply.

Steps

1. If you are not using the Internet over a *LAN*, connect to
   your *ISP*. Start the Internet Mail program by choosing
   Start, Programs, Internet Mail.

2. To check your mailbox for new messages, click the Send
   and Receive button, or choose Mail, Send and Receive
   from the menu.

3. To read a message you downloaded, double-click the
   message icon or subject line. You can use the toolbar
   buttons or the menu options to reply to the sender only,
   reply to everyone who received the message, or forward
   the message to someone else.

   If you want to attach a file with your response, choose
   the Insert File button on the toolbar, or simply drag the
   file from Explorer into the message body. Then click the
   Send button or use the menu option Mail, Send and
   Receive.

4. You can create new messages by clicking the New
   Message toolbar button or choosing Mail, New Message.
   Enter the address(es) of the receiving parties, the
   address(es) of the parties to be copied, and the subject.
   Type your message into the body.

5. Most e-mail clients will not send your messages immediately. After you have written all your messages and

responses, click the Send and Receive button, or choose Mail, Send and Receive to upload your messages to the mail server.

TIP If you are charged long distance or billed for cumulative Internet access time, choose an e-mail client that lets you disconnect from the Internet while your read and write your e-mail. Then you only need to be connected to download messages you have received and upload messages you are sending.

Internet: Using Ping

The Ping utility lets you see if a computer is awake on the Internet. It is like roll call in elementary school. You simply call out a computer's name or address and wait for a reply. Although this isn't a very interesting use of the Internet, it is a useful troubleshooting tool. If your Web browser won't work, you can use Ping to determine if the problem lies with the browser, the site you're trying to access, or your Internet connection.

Steps

1. Establish an Internet connection either over a *LAN* or with an *ISP*.

2. Open an MS-DOS prompt by choosing Start, Programs, MS-DOS Prompt.

3. At the prompt, type **ping <address>**, where *address* is the name or *IP address* of the computer you want to ping.

4. If the machine is out there and your Internet connection is working, you will receive a reply back from the machine you pinged. It will look something like this:

```
Microsoft(R) Windows 95
    (C)Copyright Microsoft Corp 1981-1996.

C:\>ping mcp.com

Pinging mcp.com [206.246.150.10] with 32 bytes of data:

Reply from 206.246.150.10: bytes=32 time=174ms TTL=253
Reply from 206.246.150.10: bytes=32 time=144ms TTL=253
```

COMMUNICATIONS

```
Reply from 206.246.150.10: bytes=32 time=170ms
➡TTL=253
Reply from 206.246.150.10: bytes=32 time=145ms
➡TTL=253

C:\>
```

TROUBLESHOOTING **If I ping the actual IP address of a location, I receive a reply; but if I type the name (like www.microsoft.com), I receive an error message or a request timed out.** The Internet uses computers called *Domain Name Servers (DNS)* to translate the alphanumeric name used in a Web or e-mail address into the IP address the name represents. If your DNS is down or slow, you will not be able to ping a location by name, but you could ping a location by its IP address. A quick way to tell if the problem really is your DNS, is to ping it. You can find the IP address for your DNS by choosing Start, Settings, Control Panel; double-clicking Network, selecting TCP/IP, clicking the Properties button, and selecting the DNS tab.

Depending on how your system is configured, the DNS information might not be at the location specified above. Another way to check it is to click Start, Programs, Accessories and Dial-up Networking. Right-click your connection and select Properties from the shortcut menu. On the Server Types tab, check the TCP/IP check box near the bottom and click the TCP/IP Settings button. If the Specify Name Server Addresses option is selected, the Primary DNS and Secondary DNS addresses should be displayed.

Internet: Using Telnet

Telnet lets you connect directly to another machine over the Internet. Then you can transfer files, run applications, or leave messages.

Steps

1. Establish an Internet connection either over a *LAN* or with an *ISP*.

2. Start Telnet by choosing Start, Run. In the Open box enter **Telnet**.

3. Open the Connect menu and choose Remote System. Enter the Host Name or *IP address* of the machine you want to connect with, choose the correct Terminal Type, and click the Connect button.

Internet Explorer 3.0: Adding an URL to Favorites

Internet Explorer lets you access the Internet through the World Wide Web (WWW). WWW sites all have an address known as a Uniform Resource Locator (URL). Typing in a really long *URL* can become tiresome, especially if you visit a particular site often. Worse yet is trying to remember a really long URL. Just like speed dial on your phone, Internet Explorer offers a Favorites list where you can store you favorite sites, then access any favorite site by simply choosing it from your list.

Steps

1. Load the page you would like to add to your Favorites list according to the directions in the task "Internet Explorer 3.0: Browsing the Web."

2. Choose Favorites, Add to Favorites. You can enter a different name for the link or just press OK.

3. Whenever you want to revisit a favorite location, choose Favorites, and select the link.

TROUBLESHOOTING **When I choose my favorite link for the XYZ Company, rather than the XYZ home page, I get a message 404 URL NOT FOUND.** The XYZ Web site may be temporarily down and you need to try again later. The Web site may have moved (have a different *URL*), or the Web site may be permanently gone. If you try a day or two later and get the same message, use your browser's Search utility to access a search engine and look for the company's page again.

Internet Explorer 3.0: Browsing the Web

The World Wide Web makes exploring the Internet a simple matter of mouse clicks. Internet Explorer 3.0 lets you click your way across the Internet while supporting many advanced Web features such as live audio, scrolling screens, and even real time interactive games. You can use the information you find on the Internet for research, business, or just plain entertainment.

 TIP Check Help, About Internet Explorer. If it is not version 3.01a or higher, you can get a free update on Microsoft's WWW site at **www.microsoft.com**.

Steps

1. Start Internet Explorer by choosing Start, Programs, Internet Explorer; or double-click its icon on the desktop. If you do not have a dedicated connection to the Internet (a LAN connection), Windows 95 will automatically use dial-up networking to connect to the Internet for you.

2. Internet Explorer will load your predefined *home page*; this is Microsoft's home site by default. You can begin your browsing from there. Even if the page didn't completely finish loading, you can click any link to continue.

    You can also choose a location from your list of favorites by opening the Favorites menu and choosing the appropriate link.

    You can also enter a site address directly into the Address box and press Enter. If you see a row of link buttons instead of the Address text box, click the Address button to the left of the links.

    If you are not sure where to find some information, click the Search button.

3. If you want to return to a previous page, click the Back button. If you've backed up several pages and want to

return to the page you were at last, click the Forward button.

Internet Explorer 3.0: Configuring

Internet Explorer lets you access the Internet through the World Wide Web (WWW). You can change many options in Internet Explorer 3.0 so that it suits your personal needs. For example, you may want to change the color of links you have visited. Or, if you are concerned about security you may want to turn on warnings when entering an unsecured site. You can change the options at any time whether you are connected to the Internet or not.

TIP You should make sure to download a patch for Internet Explorer (ie301upd.exe) that fixes a potential security risk. You can get this at **www.microsoft.com**.

Steps

1. Start Internet Explorer by choosing Start, Programs, Internet Explorer; or double-click its icon on the desktop. Choose View, Options.

2. From here you can configure whether or not pictures are shown automatically, what colors links will be, what Internet Mail program to use, and much more. Once you have Internet Explorer configured as you like, click the OK button.

TIP If you don't have time to wait for graphics to download and display (or you just don't like to wait), uncheck the General option to Show Pictures.

CAUTION The Internet contains adult material that you may not want young children to view. Some Internet sites have started rating their material. Internet Explorer will allow you to prevent access to sites with questionable ratings or sites that are un-rated. You can Enable Ratings under the Security tab.

COMMUNICATIONS

Internet Explorer 3.0: Saving Graphics or Backgrounds

Internet Explorer lets you access the Internet through the World Wide Web (WWW). The World Wide Web is full of interesting graphics. Internet Explorer will allow you to save these graphics for your own use with a few simple mouse clicks.

Steps

1. Load the page that contains the graphic or background you like according to the instructions in the task "Internet Explorer 3.0: Browsing the Web."

2. Right-click the graphic or background and choose Save Background As or Save Picture As.

3. The dialog box that appears allows you to give the graphic or background a name, and specify where you want to save it.

TIP   If you find a graphic or background you would like to use as your Window's wallpaper, simply right-click it and choose Set as Wallpaper.

Internet Explorer 3.0: Viewing an HTML Source

Internet Explorer lets you access the Internet through the World Wide Web (WWW). WWW pages are really nothing more than a set of text instructions your Web browser inter-prets. These instructions are based on Hypertext Markup Language (HTML). If you are planning to build your own Web site, looking at the HTML source for your favorite pages can be a great way to learn how to write your own HTML source files.

Steps

1. Load the page that contains the HTML source you would like to review according to the instructions in the task "Internet Explorer 3.0: Browsing the Web."

2. Choose View, Source.

3. This will open the HTML text file in a notepad. You can use the editor's Save feature to save the source file.

Microsoft Mail: Configuring

Microsoft Mail is a mail service that allows you to send and receive e-mail across your LAN. You can configure Microsoft Mail to suit your needs and change your options from the Mail Control Panel options.

Steps

1. Open the Control Panel by choosing Start, Settings, Control Panel. Double-click the Mail icon.

2. If you do not have Microsoft Mail in your list of mail services, click the Add button. Choose Microsoft Mail and click OK. Simply fill in the information as the wizard prompts you. You may need your Windows 95 installation CD or disks to complete the installation of MS Mail.

3. If you have the Microsoft Mail service installed but need to change a setting, select it from your list of services and click the Properties button. Make the appropriate changes and click the OK button until you are returned to the Control Panel.

Microsoft Mail: Creating a Postoffice

If you don't already have e-mail on your network or you want to set up your own e-mail system, you first need to create a Postoffice. Just like a real post office, the Microsoft Mail Postoffice funnels messages from one person to another.

Steps

1. Open the Control Panel by choosing Start, Settings, Control Panel. Double-click the Microsoft Mail Postoffice icon. Complete the steps specified by the wizard to create a new Postoffice.

2. Add users to your Postoffice by repeating Step 1, but choose to administer the Postoffice rather than create a new one.

COMMUNICATIONS

3. Start Windows Explorer by choosing Start, Programs, Windows Explorer. Locate the folder of your Postoffice and make it shared. (For information on sharing folders, see "Sharing: Files on a Network" in the "Networking" part of this book.)

Microsoft Mail: Using the Workgroup Postoffice

Microsoft Mail allows you to create a *Workgroup* Postoffice, which you can use a to send and receive mail with other users in the workgroup.

Steps

1. Configure MS Exchange to use the Workgroup Postoffice by choosing Start, Settings, Control Panel; then double-click the Mail icon. (See "Internet: Configuring Windows Internet Mail" for more details.)

2. If you already have MS Mail configured for network e-mail, you'll want to make a new profile by clicking the Show Profiles button. Then click the Add button to create a new profile. Add Microsoft Mail to your new profile and enter your Workgroup Postoffice location when prompted.

3. If you don't have MS Mail installed and configured, click the Add button and choose MS Mail. When the wizard asks you for your Postoffice location, enter the location of your Workgroup Postoffice.

4. Under the Show Profiles button, select your workgroup profile as the profile used when MS Exchange starts. Then restart Exchange for the changes to take effect.

NOTE Don't forget that you must change back to your network profile to check your regular network e-mail. ■

MS Exchange: Adding Groups to the Personal Address Book

(Please see "Internet: Configuring Windows Internet Mail" before you proceed with this task.) Microsoft Exchange is a communications program that can send and receive electronic messages, as well as faxes, through different services. Exchange will let you create custom groups that hold multiple e-mail addresses, so the next time you need to send the entire group a message, you simply type in the group name rather than each individual's name. Please see the Note in the section "Internet: Configuring Windows Internet Mail" if you are confused by the Exchange/Windows Messaging System terminology.

Steps

1. Start Exchange by choosing Start, Programs, MS Exchange. Open your Address Book by choosing Tools, Address Book. Choose your personal Address Book from the Show Names From The drop-down list.

2. Choose File, New Entry. Then choose Personal Distribution List and click OK.

3. In the Name box, type in the name of the group, for example, ball team, lunch group, and so on.

4. Click the Add/Remove Members button. Select the names of people you want in the group from the list of names on the left. Add the names to the group by clicking the Members button. If you want to remove a member, highlight the person's name in the right box and press the Delete key.

5. Click the OK button and close the Address Book.

MS Exchange: Adding Names to the Exchange Address Book

(Please see "Internet: Configuring Windows Internet Mail" before you proceed with this task.) The Exchange Address Book is a handy way of keeping track of everyone's addresses and has the added benefit of being able to determine a person's display name. The next time you want to e-mail **someone@long.domain.com**, you could just type **someone** or whatever you choose as the display name.

COMMUNICATIONS

Steps

1. Open Exchange by choosing Start, Programs, MS Exchange or double-clicking the Inbox on the desktop. Then choose Tools, Address Book.

2. In the Show Names From The box, choose your personal Address Book. Then choose File, New Entry. Choose the type of entry you are adding and click OK. For this example, choose Internet Mail.

3. Type the name you want shown in your Address Book for the display name. Type in the actual e-mail address in the E-Mail Address box.

   You can also click the other tabs and add additional information about the new entry, such as business address, fax number, phone number, and other useful information. Once you've added all the information, click the OK button.

4. Now you can add another entry by returning to Step 1, or exit the Address Book.

 TIP Internet and even network e-mail addresses can be cryptic. You can make it easier to remember a person's address by making the display name the actual person's name.

MS Exchange: Creating a Mail Message

(Please see "Internet: Configuring Windows Internet Mail" before you proceed with this task.) You can use Microsoft Exchange to create all your mail messages and take advantage of features like spell checking and formatting tools. You can also attach files or other objects and send those with your message.

Steps

1. Start Exchange by choosing Start, Programs, Microsoft Exchange, or double-clicking the Inbox on your desktop. Click the New Message button or choose Compose, New Message.

2. Enter the address of the recipient(s) in the TO: box, and the address of anyone you want to receive a carbon copy into the CC: box. Separate multiple addresses with a semicolon (;).

You can also select names from your Address Book by clicking the Address Book button on the toolbar or choosing Tools, Address book. The names of the people in the Address Book will be displayed on the right. Select the name(s) of whomever you want to send the message to and click the To button. Select the name(s) of whomever you want to send a carbon copy of the message to and click the CC button.

Perhaps the easiest way to access the Address Book is to simply click the To or Cc buttons next to their appropriate fields in the New Message box.

3. Enter the subject of the message in the Subject box, then click in the main message area. Type your message in the message area.

4. If you want to attach a file, another message, or an object, open the Insert menu and choose the appropriate option. Then select the file, message, or object and click the OK button.

5. After your message is complete, place it in the Outbox by clicking the Send button, or by choosing File, Send.

NOTE   Your messages will stay in the Outbox until Exchange checks for new messages, or you manually tell Exchange to deliver the message(s). (See also "MS Exchange: Sending a Message.") ▪

TIP   Microsoft Exchange will default to check the spelling of a message each time a message is sent.

COMMUNICATIONS

MS Exchange: Installing After Windows Is Installed

(Please see "Internet: Configuring Windows Internet Mail" before proceeding with this task.) If you chose not to have Microsoft Exchange installed during your initial installation of Windows 95, you don't have to redo the entire installation. You can use the Control Panel's Add and Remove Programs to install the missing pieces. (See "Windows Components: Adding and Removing" in the "Customizing Windows 95" part of this book.)

Steps

1. Open the Control Panel by choosing Start, Settings, Control Panel. Double-click the Add/Remove Programs icon.

2. Choose the Windows Setup tab. Check the Microsoft Exchange box to install all parts of Exchange. You can also select Microsoft Exchange and click the Details button to check only the portions of Exchange you want installed.

3. Close the Add/Remove Programs dialog box by clicking OK. Then, simply follow the instructions to complete the installation. You may need your Windows 95 CD or installation disks to complete the installation.

MS Exchange: Installing During Windows Setup

(Please see "Internet: Configuring Windows Internet Mail" before proceeding with this task.) When you install Windows 95 you will be asked whether or not you want to install a variety of different options. Having Microsoft Exchange installed automatically is simply a matter of selecting it during the installation. (See "Setup: Installing Windows 95" in the "Windows 95 Basics" part of this book for more details.)

Steps

1. Start the Windows 95 installation by running setup from the installation disks or CD. Answer the questions asked by the Setup Wizard.

2. When the Setup Wizard asks you to choose the accessories you want to install, make sure Microsoft Exchange is checked.

MS Exchange: Reading a Message

(Please see "Internet: Configuring Windows Internet Mail" before proceeding with this task.) Just like you used to check your mail box in the hopes that the mail carrier delivered something interesting, you may soon find yourself checking your MS Exchange Inbox to see if anyone has sent you anything interesting. When that interesting e-mail does arrive, you'll want to hurry and read it.

Steps

1. Start Exchange by choosing Start, Programs, Microsoft Exchange or double-clicking the Inbox on the desktop.

2. Open the folder that contains the message you would like to read. Select the message and double-click it.

3. Attachments will be displayed as icons within the message, you can open an attachment by double-clicking its icon.

NOTE In order to open an attachment, its file type must be registered. (See also "File Types: Registering" in the "Disk and File Management" part of this book for more details.) ▓

NOTE New messages will automatically be stored in the Inbox folder. ▓

MS Exchange: Sending a Message

(Please see "Internet: Configuring Windows Internet Mail" before proceeding with this task.) You can send messages to anyone on the network or Internet with Microsoft Exchange. Simply compose your message, add your attachments, and upload it to the mail server for delivery.

COMMUNICATIONS

Steps

1. Start Exchange by choosing Start, Programs, Microsoft Exchange or double-clicking the Inbox on your desktop.

2. Compose your message(s) according to the steps in the task "MS Exchange: Creating a Mail Message."

3. If you are not already connected to the network or the Internet, you will be prompted to connect automatically when you choose Tools, Deliver Now.

MS Exchange: Setting User Profiles

(Please see "Internet: Configuring Windows Internet Mail" before proceeding with this task.) If you have an e-mail account for work and an e-mail account for personal use; or if you share your computer with other family members who have their own e-mail, you need separate user profiles. Profiles store settings specific to an e-mail configuration. Separate profiles allow you to easily switch to the correct set of settings for the account you want to access.

Steps

1. Open the Control Panel by choosing Start, Settings, Control Panel. Double-click the Mail icon.

2. Click the Show Profiles button. If you need an additional profile, click the Add button and let the wizard guide you through setting up a new profile.

3. If you need to change a setting within a specific profile, select it from the list and click the Properties button. Click OK after you have made the changes. If you have version B of Windows 95 see the Note following these steps.

4. Select which profile you want to use from the When Starting Microsoft Exchange, Use this Profile drop-down list. Click OK.

5. If Exchange is running, you must restart it to use a new or different profile.

NOTE In version B of Windows 95, completing Step 3 brings up a dialog box for Windows Messaging Settings Properties. Select a service from the list and click Properties again. Make desired changes and choose OK twice to return to the Mail menu. ■

MS Exchange: Using Inbox

(Please see "Internet: Configuring Windows Internet Mail" before proceeding with this task.) Microsoft Exchange is a communications program that can send and receive electronic messages through different services, as well as faxes through your modem. The Exchange Inbox is the collection center for your e-mail messages and faxes. Anytime a new e-mail message or fax is received it is stored in the Inbox.

Steps

1. Start Exchange by choosing Start, Programs, Microsoft Exchange or double-clicking the Inbox on the desktop.

2. Open your personal folders by double-clicking the personal folders icon. Open your Inbox by double-clicking the Inbox icon. Any new message you receive will be stored in the Inbox.

MS Fax: Configuring

If you need to change your fax number, cover sheet, and so on, you can change the Microsoft Fax options to fit your current needs.

Steps

1. Open the Control Panel by choosing Start, Settings, Control Panel. Double-click the Mail and Fax icon.

2. From the list of services choose Microsoft Fax and click the Properties button.

3. Make the appropriate changes, then click OK until you are returned to the Control Panel.

COMMUNICATIONS

MS Fax: Installing

Microsoft Fax is a fax service that allows you to send and receive faxes with your fax modem. If you didn't choose to install Microsoft Fax when installing Windows 95, you can add it later without redoing the Windows 95 installation.

NOTE Not all modems are fax-compatible. Check your hardware documentation to verify. ▦

Steps

1. Open the Control Panel by choosing Start, Settings, Control Panel. Double-click the Add/Remove Programs icon.

2. Choose the Windows Setup tab. Check the Microsoft Fax box to install all of the Microsoft Fax components. If you only want to install some of the components, select Microsoft Fax, click the Details button, and check the components you want.

   If Exchange has not yet been installed, Windows will advise the user that it will be because Exchange is required to use MS Fax with version A of Windows 95. If you have version B of Windows 95, there are no individual components of MS Fax to select.

3. Click OK until you are returned to the Control Panel. You may need to insert your Windows 95 installation CD or disks to complete the installation.

MS Fax: Receiving and Viewing Faxes

You don't have to have a fax machine to receive faxes, so you can stay home from the office and still receive that important fax! This is accomplished in much the same way as receiving an e-mail message. In fact, the fax ends up in your Inbox.

Steps

1. Prepare your computer to receive a fax by choosing Start, Programs, Microsoft Exchange or double-clicking

the Inbox on your desktop. Choose Tools, Microsoft Fax Tools, and then choose Options.

2. Select the Modem tab, select your fax/modem by clicking it, and click the Properties button. In the Answer Mode box, choose Answer After and set the number of rings. Click OK until you are back at your Inbox.

3. When the phone rings, Microsoft Fax will wait the number of rings you specified, then answer the call. It will store the received fax in your Inbox.

4. To view the fax, go to the Windows Messaging Inbox and double-click the fax you want to view.

TIP If the line you use for incoming faxes is primarily a voice line with just an occasional fax, choose Manual as your Fax Modem Answer Mode. Then when the phone rings, Microsoft Fax will prompt you and ask if it should answer the phone or not. If you are expecting a fax, click Yes; if you are not, click No and answer the phone yourself.

MS Fax: Sending a File

If you have a document you want to fax to someone, you can save paper by faxing it directly from your computer.

Steps

1. Start the Compose New Fax Wizard by choosing Start, Programs, Accessories, Fax, Compose New Fax.

2. As prompted, supply all recipient information, choose a *cover page*, and type any desired message.

3. After you are asked to type in a message, the Wizard will ask if you would like to send any files. Click the Add File button, select the file you want to fax, and click the Open button. You can add additional files by repeating this step.

4. Once you've selected the file(s), click the Next button and then the Finish button to send the fax.

MS Fax: Sending a Quick Message

Microsoft Fax allows you to use the fax capabilities of your modem to send a fax. You simply supply the Fax Wizard with the recipient's fax number and your message and Microsoft Fax will take care of the rest. It will even try to resend the fax if the number is initially busy!

Steps

1. Start the Compose Fax Wizard by choosing Start, Programs, Accessories, Fax, Compose New Fax.

2. When prompted, supply the Wizard with the recipient's name, number, and other information. After you have answered all the questions, click the Finish button.

MS Fax: Using Cover Page Editor

If you would like your own custom fax *cover page*, with your company logo or other pertinent information, you can create one. Save your custom cover page so you will be able to select it in the Compose Fax Wizard the next time you send a fax.

Steps

1. Open the Cover Page Editor by choosing Start, Programs, Accessories, Fax, Cover Page Editor.

2. You can include whatever recipient information you want on your cover page by choosing Insert, Recipient, and selecting the applicable field. The field will be placed in the middle of the cover page, but you can reposition it by dragging it to a new position and dropping it there.

   Simply repeat this process for any Sender or Message information you want included on your cover page.

3. You can also add bitmap images or other objects by choosing Insert, Object. If you are creating a new object, select the type from the list and click OK. If you just want to include an object from a file, choose the Create From File button and enter the file name, or choose the Browse button to select the file and click OK. You can

reposition the object by dragging it to a new position and dropping it there.

4. You can use the tools on the drawing toolbar to add custom text, boxes, shapes, or lines. Simply choose the appropriate button, then click its starting position and ending position on the cover page. If you misplace the item, you can reposition and resize it.

5. After you have finished creating your cover page, save it by choosing File, Save or Save As, entering the cover page name, and clicking OK. If you save the file in the Windows folder, it will automatically be displayed as a cover page selection when you use the Compose New Fax Wizard.

Online Services: Using Microsoft Network

If you don't have access to the Internet through your network, or you don't have an *Internet Service Provider* and don't know how to get one, don't despair. Windows 95 comes complete with the Microsoft Network, a national network to provide Internet access to Windows users.

Steps

1. If you didn't install the Microsoft Network when you installed Windows 95, install it now. Open the Control Panel by choosing Start, Settings, Control Panel. Double-click the Add/Remove Programs icon and click the Windows Setup tab. Check the Microsoft Network box and click OK. You may need your Windows 95 installation CD or disks to complete the installation.

2. If you haven't already signed up with the Microsoft Network, you can do so by double-clicking the Microsoft Network icon on the desktop. Click OK in the first dialog box and follow the directions for signing up.

3. After you've signed up, you can access the Microsoft Network by double-clicking the Microsoft Network icon on your desktop.

COMMUNICATIONS

Phone Dialer: Dialing

The phone dialer is an automatic dialing application. Use it to dial common numbers or just to avoid the hassle of holding the phone while you dial and wait for someone to answer.

Steps

1. Start the phone dialer by choosing Start, Programs, Accessories, Phone Dialer.

2. If you haven't dialed the number before, enter it in the Number to Dial box. If you have dialed the number before, you can select it from the drop-down list. Click the Dial button when you are ready to make the call.

3. If you have a number you call often, you can enter it into one of the speed dial buttons. Simply click the button you want to set, enter the name and number, and then click Save or Save and Dial. The next time you want to call that number, you need only click its speed dial button.

4. If you need to make changes to one of your speed dial settings, choose Edit, Speed Dial. Select the button you want to edit, enter the new name or number, and click the Save button.

Networking

A network allows you to join computers together so that users can share resources and information. Networks are useful because you don't have to provide the same resource to each and every person. You put a resource in one location, share it on the network, and all network users can take advantage of the resource. Networks also allow users to communicate with each other through services like electronic mail.

You need several things for a network to work. The simplest networks require that each computer, or *workstation*, on the network have a network adapter card and a physical connection between the machines. The manner in which you wire the machines together defines the network *topology*. A complex network may have dedicated computers that run special networking software on multiple processors, contain massive storage space, support numerous peripherals connected, and provide network resources to network users across the company.

Whatever your network configuration, Windows 95 has the support you need to access your resources. It provides all the underlying software you need to communicate with the network, as well as handy utilities to make networking easy. In addition, Windows 95 even provides a networking solution for small workgroups so that you don't have to invest money into *servers* and software if you don't need them.

Finding a Computer on a Network

Workstations and *servers* on a network can be identified by their names, but even if you know a computer's name, you may still have difficulty locating that computer on the network. The Windows 95 Find utility can help you locate different computers on a network. This is a handy feature if you know the name or partial name of the computer, but don't know the name of the computer's workgroup.

Steps

1. Start the Find utility by choosing Start, Find, Computer.

2. Type the computer name into the Named box, then click the Find Now button.

3. Any computer with a matching name will appear in a box below the Named field. Double-click the computer you want to access.

TIP You can use DOS wildcard characters in the computer name if you are not exactly sure what the computer's name is. Use an * in place of 0 or multiple characters and a ? in place of single characters.

Identifying the Primary Network Logon

The primary network logon determines which network will validate your logon and enable you to use the network. When Windows 95 starts it will prompt you for a name, password, and possibly *domain name* or other information.

Steps

1. Open the Control Panel by choosing Start, Settings, Control Panel. Double-click the Network icon.

2. Locate the Primary Network Logon list box. Select the network you want to have as your primary network and click OK.

TIP You can also access the network settings by right-clicking the Network Neighborhood icon on the desktop. In the menu that appears choose Properties.

TROUBLESHOOTING I type my user name and password, but I am not actually connected to the network. If your primary network is set to Windows but you connect to several networks, like a Windows and a Novell, you may not receive any error messages from the other network. So, when you cannot be logged on to the other network, you may not know why. If you want to connect to the other network and are unsuccessful, you may want to temporarily change your primary logon to your other network to see what error has occurred. You may just be typing your password wrong, your password may have expired, or your connection may be loose. Keep in mind, however, that not receiving the messages can be a nice feature if you are using a laptop and get tired of the error messages like "server not found" when you use the computer away from the company network.

TIP If your network and Windows 95 password are the same, you only have to enter the password once when logging on. Windows 95 will automatically enter your password for the other networks.

When to Change Your Primary Logon

If you only have one network plus access to all your network resources and all are working fine, you don't need to change your primary logon. If you have more than one network and you cannot access all the resources on one of your networks, you might consider changing the primary network logon. Changing the logon will not fix the problem but you may see error messages that were previously not displayed. By the same token, if one of your networks is down or you aren't connecting to that network but you get error messages, you could change your primary network logon to a working network.

Installing: Network Adapter Card

A network adapter establishes the physical connection between your computer and the network. In order for your computer to work on the network, you need to let Windows 95 know what type of network adapter you are using.

NETWORKING

Steps

1. Open the Control Panel by choosing Start, Settings, Control Panel. Double-click the Network icon.

2. Click the Add button, choose Adapter from the list of network components, and click the Add button again.

3. Choose your network card manufacturer from the Manufacturers box, then choose your individual card from the list of network adapters. If the adapter isn't listed or you have a newer version of the adapter, insert the vendor-supplied disk and click the Have Disk button.

4. Click the OK button until you return to the Control Panel. Restart the machine if prompted.

 TIP When you first install Windows 95, it should automatically try to detect and install the correct network adapter. If you change the network card, Windows 95 should automatically recognize the change and install the correct adapter when your system is rebooted. If this doesn't occur or you have problems, you should install the adapter manually.

Installing: Network Client

A network client enables your computer to connect to other computers on a network. Today, a network system is often comprised of several different networks. You may use one network across the company for electronic mail and applications, and another small workgroup network in your department for file and printer sharing. You need to have a network client for each of the different types of networks you need to use.

Steps

1. Open the Control Panel by choosing Start, Settings, Control Panel. Double-click the Network icon.

2. Click the Add button, choose Client from the list of network components, and click the Add button again.

3. Choose your client manufacturer from the Manufacturers box, then choose your individual client from the list

of network clients. If the client isn't listed or you have a newer version of the client, insert the vendor-supplied disk and click the Have Disk button.

4. Click OK until you return to the Control Panel. Restart the computer if prompted.

Installing: Network Protocol

As in life, successful communication requires speaking parties to use the same language. In the computer network world, the language two computers use to communicate is called a protocol. You need to install a protocol for each type of "language" your computer needs to speak with other computers on your network.

Steps

1. Open the Control Panel by choosing Start, Settings, Control Panel. Double-click the Network icon.

2. Click the Add button, choose Protocol from the list of network components, and click the Add button again.

3. Choose your network protocol manufacturer from the Manufacturers box, then choose your individual protocol from the list of network protocols. If the protocol isn't listed or you have a newer version of the protocol, insert the vendor-supplied disk and click the Have Disk button.

4. Click OK until you are returned to the Control Panel. Restart the computer if you are prompted.

Installing: Peer-to-Peer Services

Peer-to-peer networks don't have computers that are dedicated *servers*, which everyone uses for storing files, running applications, or routing print jobs. Instead, members within the group can share their resources as they choose. The computers with shared resources, however, also serve as individual *workstations* and no workstation has more control than any other. If you want to share the files or printer on your machine with other network members, you need to install the appropriate service.

NETWORKING

Steps

1. Open the Control Panel by choosing Start, Settings, Control Panel. Double-click the Network icon.

2. Click the Add button, choose Service from the list of network components, and click the Add button again.

3. Choose your network service manufacturer from the Manufacturers box, then choose your individual service from the list of network services. If the service isn't listed or you have a newer version of the service, insert the vendor-supplied disk and click the Have Disk button.

4. Click the OK button until you return to the Control Panel. Restart the computer if prompted.

Why Install Peer-to-Peer Services?

If you already have a working network you may wonder why you should install *peer-to-peer* services. First, if you use a *client/sever* network and the server crashes, your peer-to-peer resources would still be available. Peer-to-peer services also let you share local resources like printers and files without the expense of dedicated servers.

Network: Connecting Cabling

Networks are comprised of computers wired together to share resources. Before you can use these resources, you have to physically connect your computer to the network.

Steps

1. Turn off your computer.

2. Make sure you have the appropriate cable for your network. If you are unsure, contact your network administrator.

3. Plug the appropriate network cable into the network card on your computer.

4. Plug the other end of the network cable into the network outlet.

TIP An *RJ-14* jack for a *10baseT Ethernet* connection and an *RJ-11* jack for a phone line look very similar. If you have both an internal modem and a network card, trying to figure out which jack the network cable goes into and which jack the phone line goes into can be confusing. Remember, the network cable connector is a little wider than a phone connector and shouldn't fit into the modem. The best clue, however, is that a modem typically has two RJ-11 jacks, but a network card only has one RJ-14 jack.

TIP If you are not sure where the network end of the cable should be connected, you should contact your network administrator.

Network: Connecting to Existing

Windows 95 will allow you to connect to an already existing network. Windows 95 is capable of working with a variety of network clients, adapters, and protocols.

Steps

1. Physically install your network adapter card according to its directions. Physically connect your computer to the network according to the instructions in the task "Network: Connecting Cabling."

2. Make sure you have the logon information you need, such as user name and password. If not, talk to your network administrator.

3. Install the network adapter according to the instructions in the task "Installing: Network Adapter Card." Install the network client(s) you need for your network according to the instructions in the task "Installing: Network Client."

4. Install the network protocols you need for your network according to the instructions in the task "Installing: Network Protocol." Install any *peer-to-peer* services you

NETWORKING

need for your network, according to the instructions in
the task "Installing: Peer-to-Peer Services."

5. Restart the computer when prompted.

Network: Finding the Right Networking Solution

Networks are a great way to share information and resources
as well as communicate between computers. Before buying
lots of expensive equipment and software, evaluate your network needs to determine what solution is right for you.

Steps

1. Determine your current network situation. If you already
   have a network in place, the simplest solution is to
   expand that network and connect your PC to it.

2. Determine the number of computers you need to
   network. Buying network software can be expensive;
   if you only want to join a few computers, you should
   consider using the built-in, *peer-to-peer* networking that
   comes with Windows 95. For this you'll need the
   network adapters and some network cables. Follow the
   directions in the task "Network: Connecting to Existing"
   and choose Microsoft's Client for Microsoft Networks
   and NetBEUI protocol. The client serves as your peer-to-
   peer interface and the NetBEUI is the protocol used over
   a Microsoft peer-to-peer network.

3. If you need to connect more than eight, but fewer than
   30, computers, Windows 95 *peer-to-peer* networking is
   still the simplest. Besides the cables and adapters, you
   may also want to buy a hub and hook the computers into
   a *star topology.* Then see the instructions in the task
   "Network: Connecting to Existing" and choose
   Microsoft's Client for Microsoft Networks and NetBEUI
   protocol. The client serves as your peer-to-peer interface,
   and the NetBEUI is the protocol used over a Microsoft
   peer-to-peer network.

4. If you need to connect a large number of computers, you should consider buying some *client/sever* software such as Novell Netware with one or more dedicated *servers*. Then see the instructions in the task "Network: Connecting to Existing" and choose Novell's Client for Novell Netware and IPX protocol. The client serves as your Novell network interface, and IPX is the protocol used on Novell networks.

Network: Keeping Applications and Data Separate

Applications are programs that you run on your computer, such as Word or Excel. Data is the information within a document or spreadsheet that you read and edit with an application. You can share both applications and data across a network. Sharing applications on the network, however, can be slow, and if the network goes down you can't run the application. So, if possible, keep all your applications on your local machine.

Steps

1. If possible, install your applications on your hard drive in their own folders. Refer to an application's user manual for installation instructions. Do not share these application folders.

2. Create separate folders for your data. (See "Folders: Creating" in the "Disk and File Management" part of this book.) Save, move, or copy data files in the separate folders and share those as you want.

Why Separate Applications and Data?

Keeping your applications and data in separate locations is always a good idea. Application folders contain files that the applications need to run, and you don't want any of those files to become accidentally corrupted. By the same token, when you open a data file you don't want to have to look for it among all the application files. On a network, keeping an application on your local machine allows the application to run quicker, and keeping data on the network allows other users easy access to the information.

NETWORKING

Network: Logging On

Once you have configured your network settings, you will be prompted to log on to the network each time you start your computer. Logging on allows you to access all your network resources.

Steps

1. Configure your computer to work with the network according to the directions in "Network: Connecting to Existing."

2. Choose your primary network according to the directions in "Identifying the Primary Network Logon."

3. Enter your user name, password, and other requested information when prompted as your machine starts up.

4. If you want to log off and log on as someone else or as yourself again, you can do so by choosing Start, Shutdown, and selecting the option to Close all Programs and Log on as a Different User.

Network: Mapping a Network Drive

If you regularly grab files from your co-worker's computer or continually need files from a folder that's buried under several other folders on the file *server*, you may want to map a drive letter to the location. Mapping makes accessing commonly visited computers or folders a simple matter of double-clicking the drive in My Computer or Explorer.

Steps

1. Double-click the Network Neighborhood icon on the desktop and browse until you find the machine you want mapped to a drive letter.

2. Choose a default folder that will be opened when you open the drive. Right-click the folder and choose Map Network Drive from the menu.

3. The Map Network Drive dialog box will appear with the first available drive letter already selected. If you want to

use a drive letter other than the first available, click the drop-down arrow and select the appropriate drive letter. Any drive that has a description to the right of the letter has already been mapped.

4. Check the path to make sure it is correct. If you want the mapping to be permanent, make sure the Reconnect at Logon box is checked. Click the OK button.

Why Map a Network Drive?

Mapping a network drive has several advantages. The drive will appear automatically in My Computer and Explorer, making it easy to access your network resource. You can then move, copy, delete, and rename files on the network drive just like any other drive. (See "Files and Folders: Viewing in Explorer" in the "Disk and File Management" part of this book.) The drive will also be accessible when you open or save files in applications allowing you to easily access your files.

Network Neighborhood: Viewing Network Resources

Network Neighborhood is a convenient way to explore the resources on your network. You can use it to find files, folders, printers, or other network resources.

Steps

1. Double-click the Network Neighborhood icon on the desktop.

2. You can see everything that is on your network by double-clicking the Entire Network Globe.

3. Double-click an object to open a workgroup, file server, computer, or folder. You may be prompted for a password; if you are, simply enter it and click OK. If you do not know the password, you need to contact the party responsible for maintaining that connection.

4. Once you locate the files you want, you can copy, move, or open the files as you would in Explorer. If you have

NETWORKING

write access, you can also delete files, create new directories, copy files into the directory, and edit the files that are in the directory.

TIP If you do not have write privileges within a directory and you want to edit a file, you can always copy the file to your local machine. If you must be able to save the file to its network location, you will need to speak to the owner of the directory to which you need write access.

NOTE If you don't know how to copy, move, open, or delete files with Network Neighborhood, see "Files and Folders: Moving and Copying, and "Files and Folders: Deleting" in the "Disk and File Management" part of this book. You can use the instructions for Explorer to perform the same action in Network Neighborhood. ■

Novell Network: Connecting with Windows 95

Novell Netware is a popular network operating system found on many networks. You can access the resources on a Novell network, just as you would resources on a Microsoft *peer-to-peer* network. This means you can use network printers, run applications from the file *server,* and share files with other network users.

Windows 95 can access your Novell network and allow you to use Novell network resources. The best part is that you don't have to change anything on your Novell network for Windows 95 to work with it. You only need to install the Novell components on your computer.

Steps

1. Connect your computer to the existing network according to the instructions in the task "Network: Connecting to Existing." Install the Novell Netware client or the Microsoft Netware client according to the instructions in the task "Installing: Network Client." Installing the

Netware client should automatically install the IPX
protocol; if not, then install it yourself according to the
instructions in the task "Installing: Network Protocol."

2. If you are using Novell 4.0 or later, you will only have
limited network support. For complete support of Novell
Netware 4.0 or later, you need to run the Novell Workstation Shell install program. (See "Installing: Windows 95
Applications" in the "Applications and Accessories" part
of this book.) After the install program is complete, open
the Control Panel by choosing Start, Settings, Control
Panel and double-clicking the Network icon to complete
the installation of Novell Netware 4.x support.

3. If you want Novell to be your primary log on, set it
according to the directions in the task "Identifying the
Primary Logon."

4. Restart your machine whenever prompted and supply
your Novell user name, password, and primary *server*
when asked.

Printers: Installing on a Network

Most people don't use a printer every single minute of the day,
so having one printer for several people makes sense. The
simplest way to allow multiple people to use a printer is to
make it available through the network. Before you can print to
a network printer, however, you have to install that printer on
your machine.

Steps

1. Open the Printers folder by choosing Start, Settings,
Printers. Double-click the Add Printer icon.

2. The Add Printer Wizard will guide you through installing
the network printer; make sure you choose Network
Printer and not Local Printer when prompted. When you
have finished answering the Wizard's questions, click
the Finish button. (See also "Installing: Adding a New
Printer" in the "Printing" part of this book.)

NETWORKING

Why Use Network Printers?

Because a printer is not used continuously, it is a good idea to share a printer among many users. You could hook all the computers to a printer through a switch box, but then you have to set the switch to your computer every time you want to print. A network printer allows multiple users access to a printer through the existing network wiring. The network also takes care of queuing print jobs from all users so you don't have to worry about setting any switches when you want to print.

Printers: Optimizing Network Printing Resources

Anytime someone uses a network resource, the computer supporting that resource must dedicate part of its local resources to service the network activity. So, if you are sharing a printer on your machine and a lot of network users print to it, you may not be able to do as much work as quickly on your machine.

Steps

1. If possible, connect the printer to a dedicated print server. In other words, the computer with the printer attached isn't used for anything other than queuing print jobs.

2. If you share a printer from your machine and find that complicated tasks are tediously slow, unshare your printer while performing these tasks. You can make your printer unshared by choosing Start, Settings, Printers. Right-click your printer and choose Sharing. Select Not Shared and click OK. When you are through with the task you can share the printer again.

3. If you share a printer from your machine but you only want certain users to print, establish a password for sharing or select a specific group of users. Choose Start, Settings, Printers. Right-click your printer and choose

Sharing. Follow the instructions in the task "Printers: Sharing on a Network."

Printers: Printing on a Network

With a network, you don't need to have a printer at every machine or use switch boxes to connect multiple machines to one printer. You can install a network printer as if it is a local printer and print to it whenever you choose.

Steps

1. Make sure the network printer is installed on your system. For instructions, see also "Printers: Installing on a Network."

2. If you are in an application and you want to print to a network printer, you can usually choose File, Print. This will open a dialog box from where you can select a specific printer and choose the network printer from a drop-down list. When you've chosen the printer, click the Print button.

3. If you are in an application like Notepad, you can select a network printer by choosing File, Page Setup. Then click the Printer button, select the network printer from the drop-down list, and click OK until you are returned to Notepad. Now choose File, Print.

4. If you want to usually print to a specific network printer, you can make that printer the default used by all applications. Follow the instructions in the task "Printers: Sharing on a Network."

NOTE In some applications, when you choose a specific printer, that specific printer will be the printer the application uses each time you print unless you restart the application. In other applications, if you want to use a printer other than the default, you must select the specific printer each time. ▪

NETWORKING

Printers: Sharing on a Network

If you have a printer, chances are that you don't use it continuously or even consistently. With a network, however, you can share your printer so that other users may use it, which makes the best use of the resource.

Steps

1. Open the Printers folder by choosing Start, Settings, Printers.

2. Right-click the printer you want to share and choose Sharing from the menu.

3. Click the Shared As button, then choose the applicable users or set up passwords as described in the task "Sharing: Resources by User" or "Sharing: Resources by Password."

TIP If you want everyone to have access to your printer, then simply press Enter for the password or choose Everyone for your user list. Be aware, however, that others can slow down your systems with their print jobs.

Why Share a Printer?

If you have a local printer and you don't use it continuously, you can share it with other users on the network. Once you share your printer, other users can print to your local printer without running any additional wires. This allows a single printer to easily serve multiple people.

Printers: Viewing a Network Print Queue

If you have a selection of network printers, you may want to check their respective queues before printing so you can choose the printer that is the least busy. Conversely, if you only have one network printer and it's on the other side of the building, you may want to check the queue after you send your print job so you don't have to go over and waste time waiting.

Steps

1. Open the Printers folder by choosing Start, Settings, Printers.

2. Double-click the printer icon for the network queue you want to check.

3. You can then view the status of all the print jobs within the queue. If you want to delete your print job, simply select it and press the Delete key.

NOTE Remember that you can only delete your own print jobs. ▥

TIP If you do have a current print job or even several, a printer icon will appear on the taskbar next to the time. To check the queue or queues that contain your print job or jobs, double-click the printer in the notification area.

Security: Establishing on a Network

A network can have many users on it at any given time and these users may have access to confidential information or crucial system files. In addition, You have probably heard of networks being broken into and viruses being planted. You want to protect your network from outside sources by establishing user IDs and passwords, as well as regularly scanning the *servers* and *workstations* for viruses.

Steps

1. Restrict access by assigning users network IDs and passwords. Force users to update their passwords regularly.

2. Make your application areas read-only. Limit data areas to the users who need the data within a specific area. (See also "Sharing: Resources by User" in this section and "Files and Folders: Changing Properties" in the "Disk and File Management" part of this book.)

NETWORKING

3. Make your system areas only accessible to qualified network administrators. (See also "Sharing: Resources by User.")

4. Run anti-virus software on the *servers* and *workstation* regularly. Keep the anti-virus software updated. (See also "Security: Protecting the Network from Viruses.")

Why Have Network Security?

You should establish network security for a couple reasons. The first is to protect your information and applications from outside infiltration. You don't want your secret recipe distributed on the Internet. The second is to protect your information and your network itself from corruption or sabotage. Your network has files that you do not want deleted or corrupted. You should protect these files by only giving access to those people who need and understand the importance of the files.

Security: Protecting the Network from Viruses

Viruses are programs that harm a computer system in some way. Some are annoying but fairly harmless, others can completely destroy a network's data. You want to protect your network from viruses by controlling network access with user IDs and passwords, and by regularly running anti-virus software.

Steps

1. Carefully assign user IDs and passwords to protect the network from unwanted users. This is especially true of networks with dial-up access. Make sure users who can log on remotely have unique passwords that they change regularly. (See also "Sharing: Resources by User.")

2. Run virus protection software regularly. You can have the software run each time a network machine is booted. Make sure you run virus checks on the *workstations* and the *server*. Keep your virus software up-to-date.

TIP MacAfee has an excellent anti-virus software as well as regular updates.

Why Run Anti-Virus Software?

Viruses can cause extensive damage to a networking system. Unless you never copy files from floppy disks, copy files from other computers, or communicate with other computers, your system is probably safe. Because this is not a reasonable expectation, you should run anti-virus software. Most software has an extensive database of known viruses and can detect and remove a virus before it becomes a problem. Remember, however, that you need to update the database regularly to ensure that you are protected from all existing viruses.

Security: Securing the Network with User IDs and Passwords

You may keep confidential information on your network that only people within your company should access. You also have system files and application files that, if deleted, could seriously affect the performance of your network. You can protect this information by only allowing valid users with correct passwords onto the network.

Steps

1. Never allow anyone without a valid user name and password to access the network. When adding new users to the system, create a unique password rather than a generic PASSWORD or LASTNAME scenario. The new user can always change it later. (See also "Sharing: Resources by User.")

2. If the *server* software will allow you, limit the time a user can keep a password. This forces a user to change his or her password on a regular basis. For information, check your server reference material for login scripting and password setting. If you are not sure if your software supports expiration times for passwords, talk to your vendor.

NETWORKING

Why Assign User IDs and Passwords?

To avoid data corruption or information theft, you need to control who has access to your network. You should only let users with valid user IDs access your network. Passwords can be used to ensure the person who typed in an ID is actually that person. In addition, you should control what valid users have access to. Not every user on a network should have access to system files, or you may have special areas for departments like payroll. You can create an area and only let a certain set of user IDs have access to that area.

Sharing: Files on a Network

One nice feature of networks is the ability to put information needed by many people into a location they can all access. If you have some files on your system that specific people need to read or even edit, you can put those files into shared folders and specify who has what rights in that directory.

Steps

1. Open Explorer by choosing Start, Programs, Windows Explorer.

2. If you haven't already, make a folder(s) to hold the files you want to share, then move the files you want to share into the folder(s) you want to share. (See also "Folders: Creating" in the "Disk and File Management" part of this book.)

3. Select the folder you want to share. Choose File, Sharing; or right-click the folder and choose Sharing.

4. Choose the Shared As button, then choose the applicable users or set up passwords as described in the task "Sharing: Resources by User" or "Sharing: Resources by Password."

TIP If you use long file names but users across your network do not have systems that support long file names (or your network doesn't support long file names), you may want to rename your files with the eight-character name and three-character convention. Otherwise, your file names will contain ~ symbols when others try to access them.

Why Share Files on a Network?

If you have information that other users on your network need, you could copy the information to a disk or print the information. Of course, every time you change the information you will have to recopy the file or print the document again. With a network you can share files that others need. That way, other users can access the information any time they want without disturbing you. If you are working on a collaborative project, you can even provide other users the ability to edit and change the documents you are sharing.

Sharing: Resources by Password

If you share a resource by password, only users who know the password can use the resource. You can have separate passwords for a resource for different privilege levels. (See also "Sharing: Resources by User.")

Steps

1. Open the Control Panel by choosing Start, Settings, Control Panel. Double-click the Network icon. Click the Access Control tab and choose Shared Level Access Control. Click OK and restart the system when prompted.

2. Once your system has restarted, select the resource you want to share. (See also "Sharing: Files on a Network" and "Printers: Sharing on a Network.") Right-click the resource and choose Sharing from the menu. Under the Sharing tab, choose Shared As. You can specify a different Share Name and add a Comment if you want.

3. If anyone who accesses your resource should have read-only access, select Read-only, then enter and confirm the Read-only password.

NETWORKING

4. If anyone who accesses your resource should have Full access, select Full, then enter and confirm the Full password.

5. If you want some users to have full access and others to have read-only access, select Depends on Password, enter and confirm a password for Read-only access, then enter and confirm a different password for Full access.

TIP   If you use long file names but users who access your files are not using a system that supports long file names, you should create a short share name. This allows you to control how the name is shortened.

TIP   If you are concerned about your password being compromised, you may want to consider using user-level access for your resources. Although this method is more difficult to configure and maintain, you have complete control over who can access your resources and what individual privileges each user has. (See also "Sharing: Resources by User.")

Why Share by Password?
Sharing information by password is much easier than sharing resources by user. You simply set up a password or two and provide that password to users you want to have access.

Sharing: Resources by User

With a network you don't need a copy of the same file on everyone's computer; and it's not necessary to have a printer at everyone's machine. You can put a file or printer on one computer, then grant other users permission to use the resource. If you share a resource by user rather than password, you can choose the individual user and select the rights the user has when using the resource.

Steps
1. Open the Control Panel by choosing Start, Settings, Control Panel. Double-click the Network icon. Click the

Access Control tab, then choose Uuser-Level Access Control. Type the name of the server that contains the user list and click OK. Restart the system when prompted.

2. Once your system has restarted, select the resource you want to share. (See also "Sharing: Files on a Network" and "Printers: Sharing on a Network.") Right-click the resource and choose Sharing from the menu. Under the Sharing tab, choose Shared As. You can specify a different Share Name and add a Comment if you want.

3. The names of anyone who can access this directory will be listed in the Name box. To add additional names click the Add button.

4. Select a user or group of users from the Name list. If you want the user or group to have read-only access, click the Read-only button. If you want the user or group to have full access, click the Full Access button. If you want to choose the list of rights, click the Custom button, check the rights you want the user or group to have, and click OK. Continue adding users until everyone who needs access is listed and click OK.

TIP If you have difficulty locating a network user list, or some of the users you want to access your resources are not on the list, you may want to consider using password-protected resources. This is a much easier method for sharing resources. Otherwise, contact your network administrator for information on the user list(s).

Why Share by User?

You should share resources by user if you need strict control over who can and can't access the information on your system. Sharing by user also allows you to assign custom rights for every user who has access to one of your resources.

NETWORKING

System Policies: Creating a System Policy File

As a system administrator, you can use system policies to control what network users can do or not do. This can save you time if you have difficulties with users changing Control Panel settings they shouldn't, removing icons they shouldn't, or connecting to resources they shouldn't. In order to enforce these policies, you must first create a policy file.

Steps

1. If you have not already, install the System Policy Editor by completing this step. Open the Control Panel by choosing Start, Settings, Control Panel and double-click the Add/Remove Programs icon. Select the Windows Setup tab, click the Have Disk button, select the ADMIN\APPTOOLS\POLEDIT directory on the Windows 95 CD, and click OK.

2. Check the box next to the System Policy Editor component and click OK again.

3. Start the Editor by choosing Start, Programs, Accessories, System Tools, System Policy Editor.

3. Create a new policy file by choosing File, New File.

NOTE   You must have the Windows installation CD to install the System Policy Editor. If you do not have the CD version, you need to contact your vendor and purchase a Windows 95 resource kit. ▓

Why Create a System Policy?

If you are responsible for maintaining the machines in a workgroup, you may find that system policies are a useful way to ensure that users don't change settings in the computer that could effect the computer's or workgroup's operation. For example, after you have all the computers on the network, you may want to disable the networking options to prevent the user from creating network problems.

System Policies: Setting

See "System Policies: Creating a System Policy File" before you proceed with this task. You can use system policies on your network to control what users can do and access. You can add users to your system, then assign each user specific rights that can prevent users from changing settings or deleting files they shouldn't.

Steps

1. Make sure the System Policy Editor is installed and a policy file has been created. For instructions, see "System Policies: Creating a System Policy File."

2. A new policy file will allow you to set policies for the default user or default computer. If you want to set different policies for specific users, computers, or even groups, you can add them to your policy file by opening the Edit menu and choosing Add User, Add Computer, or Add Group.

3. You can set the policies for a user, group, or computer by double-clicking its respective icon. Then click an area you want to set policies within, like Control Panel or Network. Continue clicking down through the sublevels until you are given the check boxes for the available actions. Check the actions you want and click OK.

4. Once you have made all the policy changes you need, choose File, Save or Save As, name your policy, and click OK.

TIP When setting different policies you may notice that the check boxes have three states: check, clear, and grayed. Checked means the policy is in place for that user; clear means the policy is not in place but Windows 95 will check the policy setting when starting; and grayed means the policy is not in place and Windows 95 should not even bother checking the policy when starting. You can save time when logging on if you leave grayed check boxes for policies you don't set.

NETWORKING

User Profiles: Creating

A computer is not necessarily one person's resource. Often, multiple users may use one computer, and a single user may use more than one computer. User profiles make sharing these computers easier by storing each user's individual preferences and setting the preferences when the user logs on.

Steps

1. Enable user profiles by choosing Start, Settings, Control Panel. Double-click the Password icon.

2. Select the User Profiles tab. Select the Users Can Customize option and check the settings you want included in the profiles.

3. Click the Change Passwords tab and make sure that a logon password, displayed as asterisks, is shown. If it's not, then enter a password. Click OK and restart the computer when prompted.

3. Each time a new user logs on to the computer, a new user profile will be created.

When to Use User Profiles

If you have a computer that is used by more than one person, you should consider using user policies. A user policy will allow each individual to start the computer with his or her preferred settings. This prevents users from arguing over background color, resolution, and other user settings.

Using Network Management Tools

Windows 95 provides many tools to help you manage your network. Netwatcher is a handy network tool that lets you see what resources you are currently sharing, who is using your resources, and what shared files are opened. You can also disconnect users, close an open file, add a shared folder to any *workgroup server*, stop sharing any folder within the *workgroup*, and change properties of a shared *workgroup* resource.

WinPopup is a messaging utility that lets users in workgroups send and receive messages from other computers or devices.

Steps

1. Install Netwatcher by choosing Start, Settings, Control Panel and double-click the Add/Remove Programs icon. Select the Windows Setup tab. Choose Systems Tools from the list of components and click the Details button. Check Netwatcher and click OK until you are returned to Control Panel. See the Note following these steps if you are using version B of Windows 95.

2. Start Netwatcher by choosing Start, Programs, Accessories, System Tools, Netwatcher.

3. Set up user profiles to store a user's personal settings on multiple computers. (For more information, see also "User Profiles: Creating.")

4. Set system policies to limit and control user access across the network. (For more information, see also "System Policies: Creating a System Policy File.")

5. Run WinPopup by choosing Start, Run, and entering **winpopup** in the Open box. WinPopup is automatically installed when you set up a network for Windows 95. It is another handy network tool that lets you send and receive short messages from other members of the *workgroup*. For example, WinPopup can send completion messages from the network printer to members of the workgroup. WinPopup must be running for you to receive *workgroup* messages.

NOTE These steps are based on Microsoft Windows 95, version 4.00.950 A. If you have version B of Windows 95, the following Note shows the correct Step 1 for this task. To check your version of Windows, right-click the My Computer icon, choose Properties, and look at the System entry on the General page. ■

NOTE Install Netwatcher by choosing Start, Settings, Control Panel and double-click the Add/Remove Programs icon. Select the Windows Setup tab. Choose Accessories from the list of components and click the Details button. Check Netwatcher and click OK until you are returned to Control Panel. ■

NETWORKING

Glossary

This glossary contains the terms that appear italicized throughout the book. Look them up as you go along or scan for any terms with which you are not familiar.

10base-T Ethernet   Uses the Ethernet network transmission standard with a bus topology that can connect up to 1,024 PCs and workstations within each branch. 10BASE-T refers to the wire, which is a twisted-pair cable that allows transmission speeds of 10Mbps.

16 Color   Up to a maximum of 16 shades of color are displayed on-screen.

16-bit OS   Operating system (OS) that only addresses memory 16 bits of data at a time, such as Windows 3.x and earlier versions.

32-bit OS   Operating system (OS) that only addresses memory 32 bits of data at a time, such as Windows 9x and subsequent versions.

256 Color   Up to a maximum of 256 shades of color are displayed on-screen.

640 × 480 pixels   Screen resolution describing the width and height of the display and affecting the number of windows that can be displayed. Depending on the capabilities of the video display adapter, supports 16 Color, 256 Color, High Color (16-bit), and True Color (24-bit).

800 × 600 pixels   Screen resolution describing the width and height of the display and affecting the number of windows that can be displayed. Displays more windows in smaller icons and text than 640 × 480. Depending on the capabilities of the video display adapter, supports 16 Color, 256 Color, and High Color (16-bit).

1024 × 768 pixels Screen resolution describing the width and height of the display, and affecting the number of windows that can be displayed. Displays more windows in smaller icons and text than 800 × 600. Depending on the capabilities of the video display adapter, supports 16 Color and 256 Color.

A

annotation An informative note or comment added to a document, sometimes displayed as an icon that represents the note. Windows Help permits the addition of annotations represented by paper clip icons.

ANSI characters The regular character set that is found on the keyboard plus more than a hundred other characters, including the symbols such as the registered trademark symbol and the copyright symbol.

application A computer program or software.

Auto Insertion Notification The CD drive icon is replaced with the associated icon of the inserted CD, and the CD is automatically run if an AutoRun program is found. The CD Player is started when a music CD is inserted. Turn off the option in the Device Manager to disable these features. This option must be disabled when writing to a CD-R drive.

B

bps (bits per second) Indicates the speed of a modem and the amount of data. One bit equals one character of text that can be transmitted.

bus network A local area network topology where all the computers are connected to the main wire of the network, giving each computer equal access to the wire. See also *network topology*.

C

call waiting   A common telephone feature that beeps when you are using your telephone and another call is coming in. This feature must be disabled when using a modem to minimize the potential for data loss when transferring, and possible disconnects.

CD caddy   A holder used by some compact disc drives to hold the CD.

cellular protocol   A protocol in a cellular-compatible modem used to control the error correcting features. This feature is important when using a modem and passing between cellular repeaters because of the signal change.

client   An application in which you can create a linked object or embed an object through object linking and embedding (OLE).

client/server network   A type of network where servers store files and allocate resources. Servers typically control who can access the information and use the resources. Servers can refuse to let computers or users into the system. Clients connect to the servers and request information or resources.

compound document   In object linking and embedding (OLE), a document containing objects from one or more other applications.

controls   In a dialog box, features such as check boxes, option buttons, and list boxes that allow the user to choose options.

cover page   The first page of a fax that provides basic information like the sender name, recipient name, fax numbers of the originator and intended receiver, purpose of the fax, and the total number of pages. You can elect to send a fax without a cover page if you are certain the receiver will know what to do with the fax.

D

defragmenting   The process of restructuring a disk so that files are stored in contiguous blocks of space, rather than dispersed into multiple fragments at different locations on the disk.

desktop   The entire screen area on which you display all of your computer work. The Windows 95 desktop can contain icons, a taskbar, menus, and windows.

disk compression   A utility that takes the information that is stored, or will be stored, on a disk and compacts it so that it takes less space to store.

Domain Name Server (DNS)   A computer that translates physical addresses into logical addresses and vice versa. Specifically, it can take the alphanumeric name for a location on the Internet, like **www.macmillan.com**, and convert it into the location's actual IP Address. See also *IP address*.

drag and drop   A method of copying or moving items by selecting and dragging using the mouse.

drivers   The program support files that tell a program how to interact with a specific hardware device such as a high-performance hard disk controller or video display card.

E

embed   Placement of an object created in one application into a document created with another application. The embedded object can be edited within the new document.

Enhanced IDE (EIDE)   An improved drive controller that is designed to handle hard drives with a capacity higher than

500M and to be used with IDE-interfaced CD drives, as well as standard floppy disk drives. Most EIDE controllers also have serial, parallel, and game ports that can be disabled if the computer has existing ports.

EPROM Erasable Programmable Read-Only Memory.

F

File Allocation Table (FAT) A table used to chart a file's name to the file's actual physical location on a disk.

file servers Computers on a network that are not used by one individual to do local work, but rather are used by multiple users on the network. Servers provide resources, control network access, store network files, and perform network processing.

full-motion videos The display of movie clips (.MOV) in as realistic a form as possible. Full-motion video uses system resources exhaustively, emphasizing the need for both a fast processor and more than 16M of RAM. Movie trailers can be downloaded from Internet sites, easily found from newspaper links such as **www.sfgate.com/chronicle** or **www. pressdemo.com.**

G

gateways Hardware/software combinations that provide protocol conversion so that two LANs with different protocols may be connected. For example, you need a gateway if you have Novell Network and you want computers on that network to be able to communicate with computers on the Internet. The gateway would convert Novell IPX information to Internet TCP/IP information.

H

high color (16-bit) Up to a maximum of 64,000 shades of color are displayed on-screen. This is video display adapter dependent and is also limited to the resolution that the display is set to, such as 800×600.

home page The default page you see when you first open your Web browser. You can change your default page so that you start each WWW session from your chosen location. A home page is also the default, or top, page for a Web site.

I–K

IDE A drive controller that is designed to handle hard drives with a capacity not greater than 500M, as well as standard floppy disk drives. Many IDE controllers also have serial, parallel, and game ports that can be disabled if the computer has existing ports.

insertion point The vertical cursor line, probably blinking, that indicates where the next entry will be made. You can reposition the insertion point by clicking the mouse or using the direction keys.

Internet Service Provider (ISP) An organization that can provide Internet access via modem or even direct lines for a fee.

IP address The unique number that identifies individual computers on the Internet. Every computer on the Internet has its own IP address.

IPX Internetwork Packet Exchange. IPX is the native protocol for NetWare and is used on the majority of local area networks.

L

legacy Older computer hardware that does not have model-specific information embedded in its ROM, requiring manual software setup.

link A connection between two files or objects so that a change in one causes an update in the other. Also, links in Web pages allow the user to quickly move to another page or area of the Web site.

Local Area Network (LAN) A network and its components within one organization.

local printer A printer attached directly to a computer.

M

MIDI (Musical Instrument Device Interface) A special attachment for MIDI-capable sound cards that is used to connect other types of digital synthesizers to the sound system for input and output. Can be used with MIDI-equipped keyboards, guitars, synthesizers, video editing equipment, and so on.

movie CDs Compact discs with video data. Usually used with computer animation because of the one-hour limit per disc, but regular movie titles are available in multi-disc packs.

multimedia The incorporation of audio, wave, and MIDI data with video data to create a program that is closer to real.

multisession CD A CD that has data or program files written to it in several sessions, such as a Kodak PhotoCD. A single-session CD drive can only access the first set of data on a multisession CD.

N

network topology The arrangement of nodes and cable links in a local area network. The categories of topologies are centralized such as a star network, and decentralized such as a bus or ring network. See also *bus network*, *ring network*, *star network*, and *star-bus network*.

O

object   A document or portion of a document, such as a picture or graph, that can be pasted into another document.

Object Linking and Embedding (OLE)   The Microsoft standard for creating dynamic, automatically updated links between documents, or embedding a document created by one application into a document created by another.

P–Q

PC Cards (PCMCIA)   Small, credit card-sized devices that are installed in special slots in computers, usually laptops and other portable devices. Commonly used PC cards include modems and network adapters.

peer-to-peer   A type of network where all the connected computers can share files and resources. Each computer on the network has as much control over the network as any other computer. Computers on the peer-to-peer network typically serve as a local workstation, as well as a network computer.

Plug and Play   Hardware that includes its manufacturer and model information in its ROM, enabling the computer to recognize it immediately upon startup and install the necessary drivers if not already set up.

PostScript   A programming language used with any output devices, such as PostScript laser printers, that provides versatility in creating graphics and text.

print job   A document sent to a printer.

print queue   In Print Manager, the list of print jobs that are ready for printing, paused, or currently printing.

property   A characteristic of a file, program, or object, such as appearance and behavior. Windows uses properties sheets to display and permit changes to properties settings.

protocol   A set of standards for exchanging data between two computer systems or communication devices. See also *cellular protocol* and *transfer protocol.*

R

Registry   The Windows 95 files that store all configuration information.

restore   Return a maximized or minimized window to its previous size. Also, return a backed-up file to its previous location, often from a disk or tape to a hard drive.

ring network   A local area network topology where computers are connected using an In port and an Out port for each computer. Data flows from one computer's Out port to the next computer's In port. See also *network topology.*

RJ-11   The type of connector used for telephones.

RJ-14   The type of connector used for *10Base-T Ethernet.*

S

SCSI (Small Computer System Interface)   An interface standard that is used to control hard drives, CD-ROM drives, and many other special devices. Commonly used in high-performance machines because the attached drives may have higher performance than models used with IDE and EIDE controllers. Allows up to seven SCSI devices to be used with one controller either internally, externally, or in combination.

serial UART chip   The chip on serial ports that determines the maximum connection speed of devices such as modems.

A 16550 UART is required when using modems with a speed greater than 14,400 bps. Internal modems have their own UART chip that is matched to the speed of the modem. External modems connected to an existing serial port on the computer are dependent on the UART on the serial card. Open the Modem program in the Control Panel and click the Diagnostics tab to check the speed of the serial UART chips in your system. Highlight the COM port and click the More Info button. The UART information may be displayed as:

```
UART:          NS 16550AN
```

server   An application that can create objects that can be embedded in, or linked to, documents created by another application.

shortcuts   The icons on the desktop that are used to start applications. Double-click a shortcut to start an application. Right-click to view and modify properties.

star network   A local area network topology where computers are connected through a central hub, which distributes the signals to all the connecting cables. See also *network topology*.

star-bus network   A local area network topology that combines features of the star and bus networks. Computers are connected through a central hub called a concentrator to connect the nodes of the network. See also *network topology*.

subkey   A component part of a key in the Windows 95 Registry.

T

TCP/IP   Transfer Control Protocol/Internet Protocol. The set of rules or standards that governs Internet communication.

transfer protocol   A set of rules that determines or specifies how data is to be moved from one computer to another.

true color (24-bit)   Up to a maximum of 16 million shades of color are displayed on-screen. This is video display adapter dependent and is also limited to the resolution that the display is set to, such as 640×480.

U

UNIX   A multiprocessing, multitasking operating system used by a significant number of servers on the Internet.

URL (Uniform Resource Locator)   An URL is an address of a WWW page such as **www.mcp.com**. These URLs follow a specification that provides a unique path to every page on the World Wide Web.

V

virtual memory   The operating system can use empty hard drive space to mimic system memory when more memory is needed than is installed in the computer. Use of virtual memory does slow processing because the hard drives operate at millisecond (thousandths of a second) speeds while RAM performance is measured in nanoseconds (millionths of a second).

W–Z

Web browser   A program that displays on a monitor the contents of Internet sites. A browser permits the user to search for and link to other Internet sites, and may also contain e-mail functions.

Web server   A computer that houses a Web site. It takes care of sending pages to Internet users as the users request information.

Windows 3.x   A 16-bit GUI (graphical user interface) program used with computers running with 80286, 80386, and 80486 processors. Minimum system requirements include the need for as little as 1M of RAM. The x indicates any of the Windows versions that start with 3, such as 3.1, 3.11, and 3.12.

Windows 9x   A 32-bit GUI (graphical user interface) program that combines the GUI interface with the operating system software. Used primarily with computers running with 80486, Pentium, and Pentium Pro processors. Minimum system requirements include the need for as little as 8M of RAM. The x indicates any of the Windows versions that start with 9, such as Windows 95.

Windows NT   A 32-bit GUI (graphical user interface) program that combines the GUI interface with the operating system software and networking software, originally independent programs. Used primarily with computers running with 80486, Pentium, and Pentium Pro processors. Minimum system requirements include the need for as little as 16M of RAM. Windows NT 4.0 was released in 1996.

workgroup   A group of computers typically connected on a peer-to-peer network.

workstation   A computer that is connected to a network, but does not act as a file server. Workstations can share information on a peer-to-peer network, but are primarily used for local processing.

writable CD-ROM drives (CD-R)   Compact disc drives that are designed to burn or write new discs (CD-R capable) in single sessions or multisessions. CD-R drives are used to create master computer discs (data and program files) and audio discs. Once information has been written to a CD-R, it becomes read-only.

Index

MACMILLAN COMPUTER PUBLISHING USA
A VIACOM COMPANY

Technical ⌐--- Support:

If you need assistance with the information in this book or with a CD/Disk
accompanying the book, please access the Knowledge Base on our Web
site at **http://www.superlibrary.com/general/support**. Our most
Frequently Asked Questions are answered there. If you do not find the
answer to your questions on our Web site, you may contact Macmillan
Technical Support **(317) 581-3833** or e-mail us at **support@mcp.com**.

Complete and Return this Card
for a *FREE* Computer Book Catalog

Thank you for purchasing this book! You have purchased a superior computer book written expressly for your needs. To continue to provide the kind of up-to-date, pertinent coverage you've come to expect from us, we need to hear from you. Please take a minute to complete and return this self-addressed, postage-paid form. In return, we'll send you a free catalog of all our computer books on topics ranging from word processing to programming and the internet.

Mr. ☐   Mrs. ☐   Ms. ☐   Dr. ☐

Name (first) ☐☐☐☐☐☐☐☐☐☐ (M.I.) ☐ (last) ☐☐☐☐☐☐☐☐☐☐☐☐☐☐☐

Address ☐☐☐☐☐☐☐☐☐☐☐☐☐☐☐☐☐☐☐☐☐☐☐☐☐☐☐☐☐

☐☐☐☐☐☐☐☐☐☐☐☐☐☐☐☐☐☐☐☐☐☐☐☐☐☐☐☐☐

City ☐☐☐☐☐☐☐☐☐☐☐☐   State ☐☐   Zip ☐☐☐☐☐ ☐☐☐☐

Phone ☐☐☐ ☐☐☐ ☐☐☐☐   Fax ☐☐☐ ☐☐☐ ☐☐☐☐

Company Name ☐☐☐☐☐☐☐☐☐☐☐☐☐☐☐☐☐☐☐☐☐☐☐

E-mail address ☐☐☐☐☐☐☐☐☐☐☐☐☐☐☐☐☐☐☐☐☐☐☐☐

1. Please check at least (3) influencing factors for purchasing this book.

Front or back cover information on book .... ☐
Special approach to the content .... ☐
Completeness of content .... ☐
Author's reputation .... ☐
Publisher's reputation .... ☐
Book cover design or layout .... ☐
Index or table of contents of book .... ☐
Price of book .... ☐
Special effects, graphics, illustrations .... ☐
Other (Please specify): _____ ☐

2. How did you first learn about this book?

Internet Site .... ☐
Saw in Macmillan Computer
    Publishing catalog .... ☐
Recommended by store personnel .... ☐
Saw the book on bookshelf at store .... ☐
Recommended by a friend .... ☐
Received advertisement in the mail .... ☐
Saw an advertisement in: _____ ☐
Read book review in: _____ ☐
Other (Please specify): _____ ☐

3. How many computer books have you purchased in the last six months?

This book only .... ☐   3 to 5 books .... ☐
2 books .... ☐   More than 5 .... ☐

4. Where did you purchase this book?

Bookstore .... ☐
Computer Store .... ☐
Consumer Electronics Store .... ☐
Department Store .... ☐
Office Club .... ☐
Warehouse Club .... ☐
Mail Order .... ☐
Direct from Publisher .... ☐
Internet site .... ☐
Other (Please specify): .... ☐

5. How long have you been using a computer?

Less than 6 months .. ☐   6 months to a year ..... ☐
1 to 3 years .... ☐   More than 3 years ...... ☐

6. What is your level of experience with personal computers and with the subject of this book?

	With PC's	With subject of book
New	☐	☐
Casual	☐	☐
Accomplished	☐	☐
Expert	☐	☐

Source Code — ISBN: 0-7897-1105-2

7. Which of the following best describes your job title?

Administrative Assistant .... ☐
Coordinator .... ☐
Manager/Supervisor .... ☐
Director .... ☐
Vice President .... ☐
President/CEO/COO .... ☐
Lawyer/Doctor/Medical Professional .... ☐
Teacher/Educator/Trainer .... ☐
Engineer/Technician .... ☐
Consultant .... ☐
Not employed/Student/Retired .... ☐
Other (Please specify): .... ☐

8. Which of the following best describes the area of the company your job title falls under?

Accounting .... ☐
Engineering .... ☐
Manufacturing .... ☐
Marketing .... ☐
Operations .... ☐
Sales .... ☐
Other (Please specify): .... ☐

9. What is your age?

Under 20 .... ☐
21-29 .... ☐
30-39 .... ☐
40-49 .... ☐
50-59 .... ☐
60-over .... ☐

10. Are you:

Male .... ☐
Female .... ☐

11. Which computer publications do you read regularly? (Please list)

_____
_____
_____
_____
_____
_____
_____
_____
_____
_____

Comments: _____
_____
_____

Fold here and scotch-tape to mail

‖''|''|'|''|''|'''|''|''|'|'|''|'''||''|'''||'''||'|'||

Windows 95 Quick Reference Shortcuts

Action	Shortcut
Getting Productive	
To start a program	Click the Start button, navigate to the folder that contains your program, and click the program
To quickly open a document	Double-click the document's icon
To select multiple files or folders	Press the Ctrl key while clicking each file or folder
To quickly minimize all open windows	Right-click an empty area on the taskbar and choose Minimize All Windows
To see a menu of available commands	Right-click anywhere on your desktop or on any item
To drag files or icons to other locations	Right-click the file or icon, drag to new location and drop
To open shared folders on other computers	Click the Start button, choose Run, and enter the path in the Open box to connect to a shared computer
To shut down your computer safely	Click the Start button and choose the Shut Down command
Getting Help	
To look up a task in Help	Click the Start button and choose Help
To get Help in a dialog box	Click the question mark button in the top-right corner of the title bar, then click the desired item for more information
To find the function of a toolbar button	Pause your mouse pointer on the button to have Windows display the button name
Printing Documents	
To quickly print a document	Drag the document's icon onto a printer icon
To see documents in the print queue	Double-click the printer icon on the taskbar
To identify and solve printer problems	Click the Start button and choose Help. Select the Index tab, search for print, troubleshooting to use the Print Troubleshooter
Using Windows Explorer	
To view your computer's files	Click the Start button, choose Programs, then Windows Explorer
To sort files in Explorer's Details view	Click the column heading to sort your files by
To move to an open folder one level higher	Press the Backspace key on your keyboard

Windows 95 Quick Reference Shortcuts

Action	Shortcut
Customizing Windows	
To reposition the taskbar	Drag the taskbar to a different location and drop
To change your computer's date or time	Double-click the clock on the taskbar to display Date/Time Properties. Make changes on the Date & Time tab
To change your desktop colors	Right-click the desktop; click Properties and make changes on the Appearance tab
To change your screen saver	Right-click the desktop; click Properties and make changes on the Screen Saver tab
To change your desktop background	Right-click the desktop; click Properties and make changes on the Background tab
To change mouse properties	Click the Start button; choose Settings, Control Panel, then double-click the Mouse icon and click the appropriate tab to change buttons, pointers, speed, and more
To start programs when you start Windows	Drag the program's icons to your StartUp folder
To add a program to the top of the Start menu	Drag the program's icon onto the Start button.
Disk Maintenance	
To increase your hard disk speed	Click the Start button and choose Help, select the Index tab, search for Defragmenter, and follow the Help instructions
To determine the amount of free disk space	Right-click the drive icon for the drive in My Computer; then click Properties
To free disk space	Double-click the Recycle Bin icon to remove deleted files
To locate the Recycle Bin icon	Right-click a blank area on the taskbar and select Minimize All Windows. Right-click taskbar and select Undo Minimize All to restore windows to their previous sizes
To check your disk for errors	Click the Start button and choose Help, select the Index tab, search for ScanDisk, and follow the Help instructions
To identify and solve hardware problems	Click the Start button and choose Help, select the Index tab, search for Hardware, Trouble-shooting, and follow the Help instructions
To identify and solve memory problems	Click the Start button and choose Help, select the Index tab, search for Memory, Trouble-shooting, and follow the Help instructions

® 201 W. 103rd Street, Indianapolis, IN 46290 (317) 581-3500
Copyright© 1997 by Que® Corporation.